BODY TALK

FINDING THE BEAUTY IN **YOU**

BODY TALK

FINDING THE BEAUTY IN **YOU**

A COMPILATION BY

ALLISON DENISE ARNETT & JAMELLA STROUD

Body Talk: Finding the Beauty in YOU

FIRST EDITION

Book design by Allison Arnett of www.branditbeautifully.com

Photography by KimazingPhotography.com

Book edited by Abiola Sholanke

ISBN 978-0-578-45652-2

Scriptures are from the King James Bible unless otherwise indicated.

TABLE OF CONTENTS

ACKNOWLEDGEMENTS

Thank you to all the brave women who boldly shared their stories in this book with the heart to heal others, you all are real MVPs. Thank you.

DEDICATION

To every human being who has felt less than, unaccepted, unloved or unlovable due to any aspect of your physical appearance. May you find affirmation here that you are perfect, loved, and perfectly lovable.

THE PACKAGE DEAL

BY ALLISON DENISE ARNETT

To love my body, you must love me. To love me, you must love my body. It's kind of a package deal. I can say this now, but not so much before. Before, my internal self was disconnected from my external self. I was oozing low self-esteem, and it made me a target for those who prey on girls desperate for love. My story is filled with looking for love in all the wrong places and using my body as a tool to get it.

I grew up in a single-parent home as the first of five children. My father was hundreds of miles away on an island in the Caribbean Sea called Trinidad. My mother did the best she could because, you know, we can only give from what we have. But even with her best attempts, I still lacked the type of attention and affection that made me feel loved enough to stop searching for it.

Daddy did the best he could too while overseas, calling every holiday and birthday to show his love. But try as he might have, I still did not receive the attention and affection I needed to keep me from wanting the affections of a man to prove to me that I was worthy.

My parents weren't bad parents. I know they loved me. So, what happened? Well this may sound crazy, but I think I failed to receive the attention, affirmation, and affection I needed because I was a good kid. I was the kid you didn't have to worry about. I wanted to be good. I was well-behaved. Didn't skip school. Did as I was told. Didn't smoke. Didn't sneak out the house at night. While I felt like I was "being good" out of fear/reverence of my mother; perhaps that was actually my way of asking for the attention, affirmation, and affection I so desperately needed. Like "look at me, I'm so good, don't you want to hug me?!?" Yeah—ultimately, because I was doing what I needed to do, or as we say in my family "handling my stories," the adults in my family put their attention on more pressing matters, and I became performance-oriented (doing things exceptionally well so people could love me) to get their attention.

In retrospect, what I didn't realize was that mine was not an affectionate household or family. We didn't do hugs and kisses and positive affirmations. To be honest, it's something we are still working on doing better today. Funny thing is, back then I didn't *know* I needed attention, affirmation, and affection, and I often wonder how my life would have been different had I actually received more of it. The world may never know, but this one thing I do know: To love my body, you must love me. To love me, you must love my body. It's kind of a package deal. Let's continue.

Most of my life, up until about the age of twenty-five, I weighed exactly 128 lbs. I remember it very distinctly. I remember it so distinctly because I always wondered why someone so skinny had a pudge. A belly. A belly, other females around me didn't let me forget I had. At the time, I hadn't had children yet, so it made no sense for me to have "a belly." But the truth is, I did. And I was highly self-conscious about it. I stayed reminding myself to "suck it in." In every picture, every outfit, and every video, there were certain phrases that repeated in my head.

Lanky.

Skinny.

Dark-skinned.

Nappy head.

Big eyes.

Suck it in!

Pretty.

These were common terms or phrases I heard from others about myself growing up. But wait— one of these things is not like the others. It's "pretty"! Why would I list this "positive" word with these "negative" words? That's how it appears right? Well, to me, they all have their consequences. Let's explore this.

Whenever someone of the opposite sex would show the slightest bit of interest in me, I was convinced it must be love! Story of your life? Yep, mine too. You see, I had no idea what positive male love and affection looked like. It wasn't modeled in my home since my father was living overseas. I received it from Daddy in spurts and at a distance. And so, I went on this journey of looking for the man that would define it for me.

The problem? Most men loved my body; they didn't love me. They saw a pretty girl with a bangin' body and wanted a sampling. And in my search for attention, I gave away more samples than was needed. I didn't know this then, but I was suffering from an epidemic that would require self-healing.

I became the woman who looked all together on the outside while feeling guilty about the low self-esteem she was fighting on the inside. The pretty girl who just wanted to be loved but to whom love seemed totally illusive. The girl with a sexy body who couldn't understand why the last guy didn't stay. I believe it was Beyoncé who stated that "pretty hurts." Well she was right. Heartbreak became my home. And pretty became my tool.

Two marriages, three children, and forty years later, I have finally come to a place where I feel confident in my body. It's been through a lot, and it's still on top of its game. I'm 50 lbs. heavier and now, I REALLY have a belly, lol, but I'm proud of my body nonetheless. My belly and its subtle stretch marks are my reminder to me of the children I've been blessed with and the pregnancies I made it through alive.

So, what changed? I learned that to love my body, you must love me. To love me, you must love my body. It's kind of a package deal. Yes, I know I've said that before, but this time I am saying it to myself and not to others. In short, it starts within. It sounds cliché, but it literally took a mindset shift. One day I looked at myself coming out of the shower in all my nakedness and I was awestruck momentarily. And this is what I said to myself and what I say to you now:

You are beautiful,
every piece of you,
even the things
that may masquerade as flaws
are beautiful.
There is
no such thing as flaws
Flaws are not real.
They are only things that make us
unique.... different.
They are
battle scars
and physical reminders
of the journey we've been through.

You are beautiful,

every piece of you.

~ Allison Denise

I learned to find the beauty in being lanky, skinny, dark-skinned, nappy-headed, big-eyed, *and* pretty. And even though my current tummy makes me appreciate my pre-baby belly more, I still love it anyway. The quality of men I attract now is different, because I love the whole me. My decisions about relationships have improved—because I love the whole me.

Realize this: God made you. He started with a canvas that was a carbon copy of His image, then he took His paintbrush of love and painted a piece of art that He would love forevermore. I imagine Him showing Jesus and the Holy Spirit saying, "Look at this. I believe THIS may be my best work yet!" Then He breathed life into you and with a proud Daddy look on His face He said it was good. You were meant to be different! He looks upon you, even now, and sees the purpose wrapped up in every wrinkle, belly roll, and melanin or lack thereof in your body. Do *you* see it? Can *you* appreciate the ONE masterpiece of a body that God has designed JUST for you? Can *you* see the value in this gift?

When we listen to our inner selves (God within), we can be affirmed or discouraged. What is the daily story you tell yourself about your body? Think about it now. Where did that story come from? Who told you you're ugly? Who told you you're too thin? Who told you you're too fat? Are they God? Do they have more power in your life than God?

What is the truth? Remember, God created you and said you were good. Not just good enough—YOU ARE GOOD. Period. It's time to remember who and whose you are. Let's rewrite that dialogue in your head and heart. Affirm yourself. What's the negative story you say to yourself? Let's replace it with a positive one. Flip the script of negative self-talk. For example, say to yourself:

I am beautiful. Yes, I am thin, and that's alright. My coarse hair makes having unique styles easy! Some women pray for the opportunity to have a "baby belly," I am grateful for mine. I know my height serves a purpose. My eyes make me stand out. God says I am GOOD and I believe it!

Repeat, repeat, repeat! Believe it. Feel it! Know it! And then walk in it. Release the shame and embrace the self-love. Beautiful, when you see the value in yourself, it will be easier to walk away from and let go of those who don't. It will be easier for you to pass that kindness you extend to yourself outwardly to others. It will be easier to teach other women and young girls how valuable they are too. This is our charge. I heal. You heal. We heal, and God's economy is better for it. You and I are better for it. Listen, this is for you. Read it whenever you need a reminder of who you are:

I am a woman
Beautiful, poised, and sweet
I've got purpose under my feet
Generations on my shoulders
My beautiful daughter, I have to mold her
My son is strong, I make him bolder
While every day I'm getting older
I am a woman
who's picked up pieces of her life
striving every day to get things right
I make beautiful artwork out of my mess
but to be honest I must confess,
I'm
in need of rest
and relaxation,
well-cooked meals, and preparation
for the things the good Lord has for me
that blessed living, bold and free,

so I…

take steps towards my healing,

forgiveness, self-love, and I'm dealing

with the issues of my past

so that my newfound freedom lasts

so I can live naked and unafraid

build my business and get paid

I am a woman remembering

that it all begins with me.

~ Allison Denise

Remember and repeat this to yourself: To love my body, you must love me. To love me, you must love my body. It's kind of a package deal.

HEY BEAUTIFUL HEY!

BY CLARISSA PRITCHETT

"Gracious words are like honey, sweet to the soul and healthy for the body." ~ Proverbs 16:24

Yes, you girl! When is the last time you looked in the mirror and said "Hey Beautiful" to yourself? I am not talking about saying this to yourself after someone else has said it to you or after you posted your best selfie on social media after seventeen takes and seven filters after you scrolled through all the "beautiful" comments you received. I'm talking about just you girl, by yourself, looking at yourself in the mirror while speaking words of affirmation to yourself with no validation from other people. Has it been a minute? A year? Some years girl? If so, let me tell you that you are not alone. I am right there with you along with so many other women in the world.

Truthfully, I have asked myself the same question I'm asking you. Not only did I ask myself the same question, I also tried writing down sometimes in my life when I felt truly beautiful without any confirmation from others. Sadly, after years of reading Psalms 139:14 that says, "I praise you because I am fearfully and wonderfully made; your works are wonderful, I know that full well," I found myself looking in the mirror and saying things like...

"Lawd really? Why did you make me so dang short and pasty!? I know your works are wonderful, but there is nothing wonderful about not being able to reach things off the top shelf, not being able to see past the windshield wipers in my car without sitting on a pillow and getting the 'short' jokes and wack comments from others as a grown a## woman....

...And Lawd, I know I asked You to shine upon me, but that included some color in my skin because you know I'm crack'in like a cracker. So Lawd, why didn't you shine on me with some of the melanin-blessed genes or at least give me the beautiful brown color from the family instead of light and crazy genes. And let me tell you Lawd, for real, I don't understand why you let me go through hell on earth growing up to have all these scars on my body seen and unseen and why I have constant reminders of it all looking at my crooked nose in the mirror every day." If you could just hear me girl!

Thinking of times that I have felt truly beautiful to write down on paper has ended up in another session of me criticizing myself. I have ended up in thinking about my life growing up in a single-parent home because my father committed suicide and I allowed that to make me feel unworthy, ugly, and not good enough. I ended up meditating on all the ugly things people have said to me over the years that I started believing to be true and have said to myself too. Like many other women from many different backgrounds, I didn't hear many uplifting words of affirmation growing up. I never felt like I had that "village" and healthy support others around me had. Suga! I even had family members and teachers ask me why I dressed like a boy and tell me I would never become much in life. Then when I tried my absolute best, I had people laugh and ask why I was trying to be better than everyone else or bring attention to myself. I have felt like a straight-up loser in the sight of others. Then I thought about all the anger I had because of it all and those I took it out on as an adolescent. I seriously questioned God about why He made me. Really, I can just imagine God shaking His head saying, "OMG! This child – I gave her too much spice!" every time I pop off in the mirror with unloving words to myself as His wonderful creation instead of speaking sweet and gracious words that are healthy for my body and soul. Can you relate?

See girl, if you knew me you would know that I have been through so much in life like many other women too. When it comes to my "looks" I have never felt like I fit in either side of my family with different cultures, in the communities where I grew up, and I have never felt comfortable in my own skin. I have kept maybe one or two close friends and kept a distance from the rest because I have also been "hit" on for the way I look in more ways than one just trying to be a friend. I have been spit on, lied on, talked about, knocked down, scared, bruised, and come back up fighting just to get knocked back down and busted up again. The ugly things that have happened to me at one point turned me into someone super sour and spicy with anger. In high school, I was on a mission to get away and leave everything and everyone in my past. I started my relationship with God and finally felt like I had the confidence to just be me. I was criticized for being a "church girl" and attempted to shrug off the opinions of others but it still stung. Then growing into womanhood, in the pursuit of finding and looking for my beauty in my twenties, I have gone through ups and downs with my weight and relationships. I have been every shape and size (except tall, lol). You name it, I've been overweight, underweight, skinny, fit, strong, squishy, and mushy.

Throughout life, I feel like it has always been easier for me to see and find the beauty in other women than to see the beauty in myself, which then caught me in the "comparison trap." You know that trap where you start looking at other women and feeling less than your best because another woman has those flawless features you want and admire? The women that are body-blessed all around with the curves, the hair, the eyes, and more so that you allow yourself to start feeling like you are not beautiful "compared to her or them." I can think of several times when I have found myself in this trap and not felt beautiful in my own skin and shape. I can also tell you all the things I have done to my body to "fix it to be beautiful." Some of the things I'm talking about are the numerous trips to the salons for mani's and pedi's, the hair color and cut changes (despite me wearing my hair in a bun 99% of the year), the makeup I really don't know how to put on so I spend wasteful hours on YouTube just get some tips and not have other women talk about my eyebrows anymore. Then there are the fad diets I did when I was a recovering sugar and carb Queen, the workouts that took hours in the gym to finish. Then, because I was either not light enough for some or not dark enough for others and quite frankly I could not stand the way white girls and some people in my family treated me, I spent numerous hours in tanning beds to try to look nothing like them. Also in my twenties, becoming addicted to looking like a fitness competitor, I opted to get breast implants so that I could "look better" in fitness competitions plus feel better about myself after a devastating breakup. Let me not forget dating a few men who looked good on the outside that I knew where not healthy for me but boosted my confidence till they left me feeling uglier than ugly with worthlessness sprinkled all over my life, including the Christian man that made godly promises but ended up putting his hands on me, leaving me feeling not good enough to marry.

It's possible that some women may be reading this with a side eye, especially those that have chosen me as a health and nutrition coach or people who are acquaintances and have never heard this before. Some may be smiling since I'm publicly sharing some of the unhealthy habits, thoughts, and insecurities I have had in my past. There may be other people who will judge and criticize me by what I have to share and/or think my reasons for not feeling beautiful are straight-up stupid. But I know that I am now past what others may think because there are women who need to know they are not alone and I want to be by their side. The truth is many women struggle with finding their beauty and have a story about how things have left them broken and not feeling beautiful. It may be scars from a fistfight, unwanted weight gain from a broken and wounded heart, a faded tattoo gotten with a distant friend, or stretch marks from motherhood, and I can imagine how much more I can add to that list.

I know there are people who think I have always been this crazy health, fitness, and nutrition nut that has it all together, but the truth is I have always been a hot mess in progress. In the many ups and downs of my life I have tried to find beauty in myself in all the wrong places and people instead of being thankful for the mix of ingredients God created me with. To add a cup of crazy to the mix of not finding the beauty in myself, I have also sabotaged myself and not wanted to be "beautiful" because I don't want to deal with perverts and hat'in ass women that have tried to hit me because of how I looked. I have also filled my life plate up with so much work resulting in not taking care of myself the way I try to encourage others to do, resulting in just looking straight up out of bed tired and satisfied with that.

I can't count how many times I have let other people walk through my head with dirty feet and allowed the words that they spoke keep me from seeing the beauty in myself or not wanting to see it at all. And I can't count the number of times I have been my own worst enemy, speaking sour words to myself. But I do know my body finally started speaking back in ways of physical pain and exhaustion. My body reminded me it can feel every negative word I held on to for years. After having three children and turning thirty-six years this year, my body finally said, "Girl, it's time to stop the madness and truly start speaking gratitude for every beautiful thing about yourself that God intentionally designed." So girl, I just simply made a decision to look in the mirror and give God so much gratitude for my perceived flaws and ask forgiveness for all the "bad body talk" and unhealthy "beauty issues" I have had trying to change me the way He created me to be. I told God that despite what others may think or say, I wanted to talk about my own mess so that I can be a message to young women who may have gone through what I have been through and may feel the same way. I told Him I was so ready to detox the B.S. of my past and see myself the way He and only He sees me, beautiful and wonderfully made. In the midst I also said, "But Lord I still may get spray tans to look and wear heels to be taller sometimes." Lol. I also asked for healing in many areas of my life, especially from my early years as a child and early years as a woman in my twenties. This year, I decided to have explant surgery (breast implant removal) because I knew the broken relationship of my past, negative self-talk, and looking for beauty in all the wrong places needed to be healed as the first step to start looking at myself through the eyes of God for who He created me to be. I stopped the excessive workouts and started eating tacos, donuts, and chocolate when I felt like it (in moderation of course!). I decided I don't want to miss out on time with my family or good food because I'm too busy worrying about looking fit. I simply want to be size healthy and happy. I made a commitment to speak sweet and loving words to myself every day, even on the days I do not feel like it. Let me tell you girl, I am starting to feel my body say "thank you."

We all may be busted, bent, and bruised, but that does not diminish our beauty one bit. The real truth is, we have no beauty to find in ourselves at all because it is already there!!! And God is waiting on us to feel it and see it with our own eyes and see it in others too! I don't give a sugar what color, shape, or size we all are — It is time for us to look in the mirror with a smile to say "Hey beautiful hey!" like every day! It is time for us to compliment ourselves and other women instead of comparing ourselves to them. As we love and accept our own natural beauty we empower other women to do the same. I pray that we all heal from whatever may be holding us back from speaking sweet and graciously to ourselves. I pray God opens our hearts and eyes wide to see our beauty through His eyes so that we can team up together and spread our beauty like butta around the world to light it up for the young women in generations to come. Young women growing up in the world today need us to show them that Instagram likes do not equate to their beauty, that they have no flaws to fix, and that it is OK to not feel like they belong in the mix.

It is time to feed our mind, body, and soul with all things healthy and good! We are all daughters of the most high King, beautiful in every shape, size, and shade of color. A world without the beautiful ingredients we all have whipped together by our Master Chef Jesus, would be tasteless, bland, and blah. I want to encourage you to speak sweet words to yourself and others, seek healthy sisterhood, and surround yourself with others that will uplift you when you are not feeling your best. Feed your mind daily with God's Word and snack on scriptures to remind yourself what God has to say about you. He said you are altogether beautiful and there is no flaw in you — Believe it girl! And make time for self-care; you deserve to show your body and God how much you love and appreciate it every day. YOU are beautiful! Write it down and read it every day if you have to or reach out to me so I can remind you! I hope to see you or meet you soon to give you some high-fives and taco about your body talk journey. Until then, smile girl and BE-YOU-T-FUL! I'm cheering for you!

KIMAZING PHOTOS

BODY TALK: SEXUAL RECOVERY

BY JAMELLA STROUD

My body is speaking. Do you hear what it's saying?

It's screaming, "Help me, will someone help me please?!"

You see my small waist, big hips, and curvy behind, but have you ever wondered what was really on the inside?

My body is speaking, sometimes screaming, even when I dress it up with the finest linens.

If my breasts could talk they would say, "I've felt inferior to women with perky breasts since losing the weight."

If my waistline could talk it would say, "I'm small, but I still compare myself to the waists of the other ladies."

If my butt could talk it would say, "It was my fault they looked at me in a sexual way when I was only a young girl."

If my vagina could talk it would say, "I was not a whore; I was a misguided little girl looking for a man's love in the wrong way."

I'm allowing my body to speak freely as I put my pen to the page. It has a right to say what it wants to say.

As I sat to write, I wondered what I would say. After all, I have already shared so much of my story, so much so that I wondered whether there is more worth sharing. Then it hit me. There is always more to give and share.

In my book "Bulimic to Believer," I revealed my story in its rawest form. I was truly Naked and Unafraid in every sense of the words. I decided to share from where I am currently in my story. First, I'm going to share some details to bring you up to speed.

In 2011, I went on a mission trip to St. Lucia that my church was hosting. I was young, twenty-eight to be exact. I was eager to take the journey across the waters to serve, to give of my time and talents, and to help someone else. I felt something within my heart pulling me to serve on this mission trip, and I followed it. That's the story I would like to be the truth, but here's the real story: I was young, ambitious, and prideful, looking for any opportunity for recognition and applause. I heard about the opportunity to go on a mission trip, and it sounded like my ticket. Now people could view me as a good person because I was going to "do good" on the trip.

Upon arriving in St. Lucia, I discovered there wasn't anything for me to do. They weren't building anything or feeding people. The pastor was only preaching for six days a week while I was in charge of running the slides for his PowerPoint presentations. After discovering what my purpose and role was on the trip, I was disappointed because my motives were tainted. "What was I going to tell people I did on the mission trip?" I thought to myself. Would

I say, "I went on the mission trip to operate the pastor's PowerPoint for three weeks?" No one was going to applaud me for that, I thought to myself. There would be no applause or honorable mention for that; my motives were all distorted. I was in St. Lucia, and there was no turning back now. I surrendered to my assignment for the trip.

One night as my pastor preached during the end of a service, he made an appeal asking for those who had been sexually active to recommit their bodies to God, to honor themselves, and wait until marriage to engage in sex again. I sat on the wooden pew on the front row struggling with myself and wondering if this message was for me. I surrendered to the struggle and rose to my feet only focused ahead. I was dedicating my body to God as a temple. I knew in that moment that my reason for going to St. Lucia had nothing to do with being on a mission trip but everything to do with a greater mission to heal my body from within. I made the commitment to myself, God, and all the witnesses in the room, and I was serious about it.

Many have asked me how I did it. Did I masturbate, did I have sexual desires, or what did I do to remain celibate? I always answer by saying it was a process like all of life is. I asked to be kept, and there were times of temptation when I almost gave up but said no. No I didn't masturbate, and after a few years I didn't have sexual desires.

I recall an incident in the early part of my journey. I met this handsome chocolate man—very easy on the eyes. We seemed to have a lot in common at the time. He was vegetarian, and so was I. He was transitioning in life, and so was I. One Saturday evening, he picked me up, we hung out, and then he brought me back home. I invited him in, something I knew I didn't need to do because I knew myself. We sat on the couch watching TV. He leaned over and kissed my neck. At this time I was on my journey for about one year and half. I moved over because it felt nice. He moved closer and did it again. I moved over again and so did he. I jumped up off the couch and went outside on the balcony. Guess what. He followed me and kissed my neck more. I was saying no in my head, but my body was having a different experience. I went back in the apartment and sat on the chase. Of course, he followed. I stopped fighting for a moment, then I said, “No, I can't do this.” He was really into it, and it was difficult to get him to calm down. It felt like he turned into another person by this time. I began to say out loud, “Jesus help me,” over and over, and God heard me. He calmed down, and I was saved from myself. Later, he told me he could have raped me because he was so amped. He also revealed his deep painful sexual trauma he experienced. Days after the experience I was devastated because of my behavior. Pride wasn't finished with me. I had put myself up on a pedestal because I was practicing celibacy. When people would ask how I did it, I would say, “Just make your mind up and do it.” I never gave God credit for keeping me, until that moment. I knew then that I was only celibate because I asked God to keep me.

In 2017, my sexual desires began to resurface. I honestly thought something was “wrong” with me because they felt strange to me. In my confusion I went to see my therapist; I needed to work through my feelings. I explained to her my story about being molested, being promiscuous, and being celibate: all the things I share in my book “Bulimic to Believer.” She assured me that I am perfectly normal and it's normal to have sexual desires. She also explained to me that the years of celibacy were for healing and wholeness, because my first trauma came through sex and my restoration began through sex. She talked about my femininity being restored and how sexual violation can shut down that part of a woman and have her to operate from more masculine energy. I totally understand her because for most of my life I was a tomboy and hid my body. I hid because subconsciously I believed it was my body's fault for the sexual trauma I'd experienced. I believed if my waistline weren't small or my behind weren't curvy I wouldn't have experienced molestation, so I hid my body and wished it looked different, so much so that I even went as far as getting liposuction on my thighs to make them smaller.

Fast-forward seven years later to 2018, I'm still celibate and honoring the commitment I made to myself and God, although my life is now taking a turn for the better. I mention in 2017 my sexual desires began to resurface. I began to think about sex and feel sexually aroused and be okay. At this point in my life, I have done so much work for healing and wholeness of my mind, body, and spirit that I know I'm entering into another part of healing. I said to God I want to experience great sex someday and not feel bad or wrong about it. I know that as I continue on my wholeness journey I will have the opportunity to experience just that. I'm currently in a relationship in which I'm able to explore my sexuality. Although I haven't had sex, I'm learning more about sex in a healthy way.

If my body could talk it would say:

"Jamella, what you experienced as a young girl did not define who you are; it helped shape you into who you are. Your body is beautiful and was built by God. Your small waist was created by God. Your curvy behind and hips were built by God. God saw you and knew the body you needed to fulfill your purpose in the earth. Although I, your body, was violated, I never gave up on finding restoration and peace. Jamella, no matter what has happened or what will happen in the future, you are resilient and made to recover."

WOMAN OF EXCELLENCE

BY MAJOR LINDA C. ZAMORA

Woman of Excellence! Not perfection...EXCELLENCE. I strive to be one, to develop them, and to surround myself with them. This is my attitude now, but I didn't always feel women were my allies. They created doubt in me where none existed before. They mocked my appearance: I was too short, too thick, too busty, wore too much or too little make-up, was too strong, not strong enough, and everything in between. This is not a story of defeat though; this is my triumph over negative influences and self-doubt that came about from the lessons those women eventually helped me learn.

Thirty-one years of my life have been dedicated to military service. I was signed into service at seventeen by my Dad since I was too young to join on my own. It was my first solo venture outside the family fold and I felt invincible. Healthy and strong thanks to the exemplary guidance of a military father, I was ready for everything. My motivation as a young soldier was to beat everyone at every challenge and not let anyone see I was phased by difficult tasks, harassment, and negative behavior from others. I had to be tougher because I was smaller, thicker, and a female. I had really short hair; I think subconsciously the more I thought I looked like the males the more accepting they would be to count me as a peer. I didn't want to be labeled "girly" because that had a "weak" feel to it. In my mind, I separated the part of me that loved my femininity and the part that recognized my physical strength and tenacity. I learned from other military women above me that femininity and strength were two separate identities that could not co-exist for me to be effective. This was the first time I had a perception of my body as anything other than exactly what it was intended to be: an awesome vehicle to take me where I needed to be in life. I felt that if other women were telling me I had to change then it had to be correct because they were succeeding in our field using those rules. I started looking at my physical self in a way I had never considered. I believed I wouldn't be taken seriously if I wore makeup, even though I love makeup. I like to joke that I'm Latina and we don't even go to the corner to check the mail without a face on! I tried to hide my curves and disguise any visible form of femininity. I wore boyish clothing and shoes and tried to blend in so much that I was losing myself, but I didn't realize that at first.

I went to military school after Basic Training. When I arrived for my first year I was excited to find an all-female Troop. All the leaders looked like some of the strongest young women I'd ever seen. I wanted to be just like them. Soon after my arrival I realized they were not examples to follow but warnings to heed. They were physically, mentally, and emotionally abusive. They were petty, jealous, and vindictive. Every scary attribute you could name, they were the incarnation. There was no acceptance, camaraderie, or anything remotely positive or supportive about their interactions with the new cadets. I understood the necessity for strict, discipline-instilling behavior, but this was on a completely different level. Near the end of our first semester, my roommate and I were preparing for a critical inspection. Everything was measured to the tiniest fraction to ensure it was in compliance. The floors were stripped and waxed, and uniforms were pressed to perfection. Around one o'clock in the morning a member of the Troop leadership came into our room and pulled everything out of closets, dumped our regulation-made bunk bed mattresses and bedding onto the floor, kicked and threw our belongings across the room, and then poured water all over everything. She was swearing at us and telling us that we were not cute and to stop thinking that we were because we were too fat and ugly to get the attention of her male peers. She was going to show us what cute girls got. When she left the room, my roommate was reduced to tears and left to call her parents to come pick her up. She was not going to stay in school for any more abuse. I found one of the adult Tac Officers (similar to guidance counselors) and showed her what happened. The offenders were punished, and the following semester the Corps of Cadets integrated females into the all-male Troops, and the situation was diffused. I thought that was an isolated event. Sadly, it was only the beginning, and I was more confused than ever. I was doing what I was taught was necessary to blend in with the males and it still wasn't right. I was still getting backlash for my looks and the perception that I was using my body to get attention. Instead of considering they were wrong I internalized the issue and started to think my own curves were my enemy. No matter what I did, my body was causing issues for me that drew negative attention.

I've been asked countless times how I deal with harassment in the military and that it must be awful to deal with the male soldiers who are not respectful. People are usually surprised to find out it is not the males who have caused the most dramatic work situations for me. I had to file a harassment complaint against another female Officer who sent me in excess of two hundred harassing, hate-filled text messages. I've seen women lie and cheat, file false claims against their female Leaders who wrote them up for poor performance, and I've seen them lose careers because they sent personal information they had access to in order to seek retaliation for disciplinary actions taken against them. I've had to mediate between female soldiers because one felt like her female supervisor did not like her because she was too pretty. I've heard the worst rumors about myself from people who did not realize they were talking about me. I've been told to wear more makeup, I've been told to wear less makeup, to cut my hair short, to grow it out, or color it—all by other women. Not one time in thirty-one years has a male soldier made recommendations to me about hair, makeup, or how I should or should not dress in order to get ahead in my career.

I finally learned that my femininity as well as my physical strength and tenacity could not only coexist but were all more powerful when combined. We have programs in the military for sexual harassment/assault and Equal Opportunity, but I believe we need one for peer-to-peer development. A program that incorporates the powerful lessons I've learned from both positive and negative females. Something to replace rivalry with sisterhood. Open a dialogue that promotes mentorship and pulling other women up to stand on the shoulders of those of us who have served and learned hard lessons for them. I want to impart to them these life and leadership lessons. I believe this program could translate easily into any organization, not just the military, because it would be built on foundational values that are universal. These are the values I finally recognized as my tools for releasing negative influences I was allowing to feed my debilitating poor self-image. They helped me heal my perception of my body and gave me the strength to thrive in it instead of hiding or changing it. These are Major Zamora's Lessons Learned:

1. "**Well Done is Better Than Well Said":** You hear "Lead by example" and Benjamin Franklin captures that sentiment like no other with this quote. We have to show others the example to follow, show them what right looks like. We cannot tell them how to be; what to wear, what to disguise, minimize or change. We must teach them by our actions, that it is amazing to be themselves exactly as they appear.

2. **We Teach Other People How to Treat Us:** When we allow people to show disrespect or any other negative disposition toward us and don't stop it, then we let them know it's okay to do it. I was stuck in that position for so long because I never told those people trying to change me or make me hide my true self that is wasn't okay to give me that poor advice. Conversely, if we send out good energy toward people or them toward us and it is well received, then we've taught them that is the accepted behavior.

3. **Femininity Does Not Denote Weakness**: If you are living the first two lessons, then three is a non-issue; respect is non-gender biased. If you are living through your positive

actions and teaching others how to treat you, then whether or not you are wearing lipstick or have big breasts is irrelevant. You will already have taught others what a leader looks like and the respect you earn will erase any idea that your femininity has created weakness.

4. **ALWAYS Choose the Hard Right Over the Easy Wrong:** I know it sounds trite, but it is absolutely true. I could have taken the easy way and left military school when things got ridiculously difficult. I'm not saying my roommate took an easy route; she took the route she was capable of handling at that time. I still consider her the catalyst for my action because I did not want another person to be reduced to tears and give up their opportunities because of others' poor behavior and opinions. I stayed, got people who could assist involved, and dealt with the repercussions so the next group of women could have a much better situation than we did.

5. **Remember *Who You Are* and Remember *Whose You Are:*** If you start with respect for yourself and respect for your family, organization, and Faith, then you have all the validation you'll ever need. I was always confused by the different advice I got from other women. Be this way, look that way, and act one way for some but another way for

others. I finally realized I already had the platform from which I needed to grow. I grew up knowing I was loved and could master any obstacle through my Faith and with the toolbox filled with values my family instilled in me. My parents were walking the talk and were living, thriving examples of everything I could accomplish. It took me a long time to appreciate those attributes as gifts and use them to rediscover myself so I could appreciate my body again.

6. **Every Next Breath is an Opportunity to Start Over....Take It!** Please don't stall your progress by thinking you have to wait for New Year's Day or Monday or tomorrow to change negative habits or destructive mindsets. There is no perfect time or situation that will present itself. Life happens, and unplanned events drive themselves onto our path, so don't wait and don't get distracted...start right now...with your next breath.

7. **Leave Everything You Influence Better Than You Found It:** This lesson can be applied to every relationship, every human interaction, and every situation you grace with your involvement—from the largest events to the smallest. I think about this when I engage with others. From the onset of interaction, I want them to feel my positive energy before we even speak. Everything from that positive outreach on, I

want to be something that enriches the engagement for both of us. I also consider this lesson on small things. When I go into a public restroom and notice paper towels on the floor next to the garbage receptacle, I use my own towel to pick the others up. I left that space a little better for the next person. Your positive influence might be exactly what someone else needs to feel better about what they might be going through.

8. **Luck is for the Unprepared:** From the time my children were very young, we would repeat this mantra to one another. We would wish one another "Success" instead of luck because we knew the time and energy expended for the endeavors was beyond being lucky. We are blessed with life and given purpose. We cannot wait for luck to intercede to drive our visions. We shouldn't hold "perfect" legs, flat abs or gorgeous faces against others because they got "lucky." We can't give that kind of power to luck. We also can't blame luck or lack thereof for our missteps. We have to own all of it, the good and the bad, and use them to prepare for our missions of excellence. We have to employ every lesson, every "tool" in our toolbox, and we have to engage every day to bring about excellence. That's work not luck.

9. **Teamwork Truly Does Make The Dream Work:** When you give people ownership and help them feel like they belong, they will commit themselves and their talents to your cause. Finding your tribe, your posse, your kindred spirits, your Squad, or your team is vital for success. If you decide you are not living in the body you are happy with and you want to change it, seek out your support from those closest to you—the ones who will commit to you and your efforts. Can you achieve excellence on your own? Yes. Is the reward greater when you share the opportunity? Definitely. Is your span of influence greater when you bring more like-minded beings into your circle? Most assuredly. Share with others! Share your gifts, your love, your energy and they will share theirs with you. If knowledge is power then shared knowledge is a super power.

10. **Positive Attitude Is Critical:** You can influence an entire organization with your attitude. That works for a positive and a negative one equally. I have to remind myself continuously that I am too positive to be doubtful, too optimistic to be fearful, and too determined to be defeated. That simple statement (from a bumper sticker...sometimes inspiration comes to you from the most innocuous sources...be on the lookout for it) drives my decision to

change the atmosphere when I feel like pessimism is creeping into my environment. When those old self-doubts about how I look or how someone else thinks I look creep in I'm able to stop them with a simple change in mindset.

11. **Be firm, be fair, and know when to have fun.** These three Fs have served me well in my career and in life in general. You must be firm with yourself. Some people call this self-discipline. This is a focus or re-focus tool. Being firm will give you the drive to achieve your personal excellence. It will also keep you on track when you feel doubt or self-loathing threatening your achievements. Being firm with others helps them see you are focused and lets them know they will not be able to deter you from your path. Being fair with yourself and others ensures everything is done the same each time and no one has to expect something different or something less from you. Knowing when to have fun is more difficult than it sounds. I believe some people get so caught up in carrying their negative banners—the hurt from previous wrongs (Victim), the guilt from poor decisions (Dumb), the regret from unfulfilled missions (Failure), the self-doubt, or loathing from someone else's opinions (Ugly/ Fat)—that they cannot look past them in order to see the joys in life. Don't abandon some of those banners, especially

the ones that add to your toolbox...like the Victim. You can grow from that hurt, but don't let them obscure your happiness either.

12. **Most Precious Gift You Can Give To Others Is...Your Time.** We are blessed with a set number of moments on this Earth. Those moments are gifts and should be cherished because they are finite and we don't know when they will end. Choose very carefully how and with whom you opt to spend yours.

Excellence is attainable for everyone. It is not measured by anyone else's standard, and it does not manifest the same for everyone. It is based on the gauge you set for yourself. That gauge is tested time and again. It is tested by disappointment. I was not protected from physical harm as a child. It is tested by tragedy; I lost a baby in between my daughter being born and later being blessed with my son. It is tested by catastrophic events; I lost my Dad to homicide when I was twenty-three years old. Sometimes those tests are internal. As I mentioned before, the banners we sometimes carry are tests. If I were so focused on carrying a "victim" banner or "I'm too fat" banner then my energy would not be available to carry all the other banners that serve me and others more. Like Believer, Mother, Daughter,

Veteran, Business Owner. I do not strive for excellence for recognition or to measure myself against anyone else. It is because my God deserves a Servant of Excellence, my children deserve a Mother of Excellence, my mother deserves a Daughter of Excellence, my soldiers deserve a Leader of Excellence, and any other soul who finds themselves drawn into my energy deserves a connection of Excellence. If I ever feel I lack motivation or get bogged down by negativity and feel that I'm not enough or way too much or allow self-doubt or self-loathing to chink my armor, I remind myself of what they all deserve and what I expect for myself and I keep driving forward to achieve that pinnacle. Please remember you are here to drive the rest of your mission in the body you are in right now. If it is not the vehicle you feel is the most effective to get you where you have to go, then change it, fix it, correct it, adorn it however YOU wish. Do not make those decisions based on what someone else thinks is right for you. Don't give others the opportunity to design your best self. I finally understood what I wanted, what I liked, what I loved about me, and I applied my life lessons and values to those attributes in order to get to where I am in this moment, and I have never been more at peace with myself, more aware of my gifts, or more compelled to share with others. Go to your destiny in the body you love and accept. I wish you the greatest SUCCESS....Major Linda C. Zamora

THERE'S FREEDOM IN LOVING ME

BY MEGAN MANIGAULT

When I think of body image, the floodgates of my mind open. How can I possibly express the true essence of what body image means to me with the constraints presented to me. Perhaps the best way I can explain it is to give snapshots of my journey and how I arrived at this place of freedom. When I think of my body today, I see it as, "in process." Some may see that as a weird word choice, but let me explain.

As a young girl, I had so much excitement about my dreams and aspirations. I smiled a lot and was very playful. I learned how to show love to others, and in return it was love that made me feel happy. The only thing I knew about my body is that it needed to be cleansed daily and that it was made fresh and pure. However, I soon learned that sometimes people you love and trust can rob you of that innocence. I also learned that without permission, individuals can disrupt your process. Some had no respect for my space or the purity of my body.

At the tender age of five, I was sexually abused. This disruption and violation continued for the next five years by more than one person. I never knew the importance of my body. I simply hated the fact that it existed. What was it about me that gave people permission to violate my personal space? Was I ugly? Was I too brown or too fat? Was I so clean that they thought I needed to be soiled? I could not figure out why I had to experience abuse at the hands of my loved ones. I went through a period of trying to change my looks. I went from the girl with bows and cute pink dresses to a girl with no hair bows, no fancy hairstyles, and no dresses...just jeans and T-shirts. I wanted to be different so that others would leave me alone and stop damaging my body.

As a defense mechanism, I began to alter my look and the way I carried myself. It was how I protected my body. To me, it was important to protect my body in this stage of the process. One day a classmate of mine pointed out to me that I looked more like a boy than the boys did. It was in that moment that I fully realized the transition I had made in my appearance. While her comment was an opinion, there was some truth in it. I had gone through great lengths to protect my body by becoming what I thought to be, "less appealing," to my abusers. Everything that occurred later in my life has been tied to experiences in my childhood. I grew up wanting and yearning for love, but in the back of my mind, I always thought someone would hurt me and/or take advantage of my body. I had a lot of trust issues.

The sexual abuse, mental abuse, and trauma of life really took a toll on me at times. I attempted suicide a few times. When thinking of my body, I reflect back to a traumatic accident I had when I was about 16 years old. One late evening on the way to an aunt's house, I got into an accident. At the time of the accident, I couldn't remember anything about it. Apparently in the ambulance I kept losing consciousness. I was in the hospital for weeks. As time went on, I started to remember things; like me driving on a narrow highway, someone hitting me, my seatbelt popping, and me flying through the windshield into a tree.

When I arrived at the hospital, I was vomiting constantly. When I would vomit, I could feel something hanging on my face. Once my parents and other family members arrived, I remember not being able to open my eyes and hearing my family crying. My parents had decided that for the first few weeks in the hospital, It was best to block the mirror in my room. I remember not being able to walk as well as sleeping a lot. I was in so much pain and I knew my face had to be bad for them to cover the mirror. I also could see the spots and cuts on the rest of my body from them removing glass out of my skin. In my mind, I was battling with my body. "Now I can't walk. I have marks, cuts, bruises all over my body. I can't see my face, unable to stay awake, and still hate myself," I was thinking. I remember going to sleep one night and in my thoughts saying, "Finally I get to die."

But, I awoke the next morning. Truthfully, we don't decide or determine death. As I would lay there, I was thinking about life. The good days, bad days, the struggles, and the triumphs. It was life that I needed to celebrate. It was the fact that through it all I still had a body. Sure, it was broken and bruised, but I was alive. I started writing, what I was thinking.

My thoughts were is that the world is full of imperfect people. Our abusers and even our enemies are all individuals still needing guidance, help, and instruction. By not allowing myself to trust and love fully, I was still allowing their imperfections to control me. It was time to get ready to make changes, not just with my inner appearance, but to be ready for what my outer appearance had become from this car accident.

I received more therapy and was finally shown my face. The feeling of horror took over me and I cried hysterically. My face had become unrecognizable.. The thing I felt hanging when I was vomiting was my skin. It had been completely separated and severed. The skin on my face was completely gone near my eyes, so much so that they had to pull the skin back together with skin grafting, stitches, and several surgeries. I was so depressed that I stopped eating. The hospital wouldn't release me because I refused to eat. I literally wanted to die. I remember them giving me my favorite foods in an attempt to get me to eat, and still I didn't want it. I felt lost again, I felt invaluable again, and most of all I felt abused again. The person that hit me left me there to die, and again I wondered, "Why me? What about me made me a target?"

I tried so hard to get to a positive space in life, and then this happens. The moment I will never forget is the aunt who I was going to see that night showed up at the hospital. She immediately says to me, "So you're not eating?" I responded, "I don't want to eat. Look at me." She replied, "Look at you. You are beautiful Megan, you have always been and still are. This moment does not define you. It's the inside we love. Now eat!" She had a no-nonsense personality, but those simple words meant so much to me and definitely came at the proper time. This implanted inspiration in me. Beauty is crafted in so many forms and isn't only defined by your outer appearance. Who are you on the inside? Who are you as a whole body? So I ate and though it took months for me to learn to walk on my own and maintain balance, I walked again. I started to feel confident that I can make broken look and feel good. My beauty was within, and it can be felt and seen outside. It was the bruises, hardships, and triumphs that showed my true beauty and ability to conquer obstacles.

It was important for me to start understanding why I would react to life's obstacles as I did. I feared the unknown. I felt safe if I could control all aspects of my life, that included others. No satisfaction came from being in control or attempting to control all things. The fact is, that's impossible. Once I realized this, I was granted a little more peace and understanding. See it's impossible to control the minds, actions, and thoughts of others. But, it is quite easy to control YOU. Sometimes we really don't realize that it is our thought process and perceptions that navigate our view on the world around us. I started to love to express The Serenity Prayer often, "Bless me with the serenity to accept what I can't change and the power to know the difference."

This prayer is so powerful, but oh so true. Control what you can and accept what you can't. I started to see that a little understanding of self could change the dynamics of life, and I had to share it with the world. Though my life still wasn't perfect, if I was granted some peace and clarity I surely was going to give it to others. I loved the quote and was making changes, but, I still needed work.

This clarity didn't mean life would be without bad days, hardships, and misunderstandings. A little over three years ago; I was going through many hardships with family members, my marriage, and some friendships. I fell back into a space where I wanted to understand the whys of individual action. It was as if I was stuck, unable to refocus because I still sought understanding from those I chose to love in life. I remember feeling really low, as low as I felt when I went through my childhood hardships. I discovered that the more stressed I became, the more weight I gained, and the more depressed I became. One day I sat quietly in a room, just me and the four walls. I thought about my life, my choices, and my circumstances. It came to me that I had put so much belief in people and not enough belief in myself. I had relied on the love of them for my happiness. I sat, thinking about how my body all around was being impacted by my actions and decisions. I thought about how my belief in making others happy couldn't possibly make me happy if I hadn't discovered how I could love and treat myself. I was living unhealthy; mentally, emotionally, spiritually and needed to become purely naked with myself. I couldn't properly love anyone else without knowing how to love myself. The neglect I had for myself was showing up in all relationships, and I wore it on my body. In this moment, it became very clear to me that I had to choose me and decide to do something different.

I remember speaking to a workmate that I trusted during this time in my life. She listened to me as I confided in her about a few of my dilemmas. Though in the process I had gained more and more clarity and awareness of myself, I still was a work in process. I can remember telling my workmate what I deserved from people and even my employer; she looked me directly in the eyes and stated, "You don't deserve anything. What do you deserve?" In that one statement I found a new perception.

I realized it had been my choice to continuously give of myself to others and not receive much in return. I wanted to receive things from others, that I hadn't given to myself and couldn't really define. Did I require anyone to respect, honor, love, or be loyal to me? How could I require what I didn't really understand? When we consider our body as a whole, we are able to view all the areas in which we need to make improvements. You may be good in one area but suck in another. If we focus on putting the work in to really get to know ourselves we would find much understanding and love there. My workmate challenged me and my brain really started searching for answers. I had to ask myself the following questions. How am I treating my body as a whole? Do I know me? Do I love me?

After this conversation, I decided to do some soul searching. I started reading inspirational books, listening to speakers, and writing; all of which were very therapeutic. It was time for me to learn to start loving me better than ever before. I had to start taking care of my mind so that my body could benefit from the healing process. Some days were good on this journey and process of really learning me as a whole. I really had to reintroduce my body to me. "Hey Girl, where have you been all my life?" This process would allow me to heal so I could truly love those God sent me to love.

I wanted to embrace those who without fail had shown me their love, even when I didn't truly love myself. It became apparent to me that I had forgotten things that I like to do and what makes me smile. So I created a list. As I completed this list, I also asked myself why I liked the items on the list and why I hadn't done some of my favorite things? It really opened me up and reintroduced me to me. This process hurt some days, but other days were amazing. It was time for me to get really familiar with who I was and love my body just the way it is. When I started implementing the list of items in my life, it started feeling good to be alive.

The world will attempt to make you believe that loving you first is wrong or that there's a certain way you should look to love your body as a whole. We are all different, there is no absolutes. We are all different and beautiful and worth the love we give to self. Loving yourself that allows you to function well. Whether it's with family, work, business, marriage, or friendships. Sometimes people will try to make you believe that your body has to have a certain look to be held valuable. If we think of our generation of stories, seeing images such as Snow White, Beauty & the Beast, and Cinderella, they were all beautiful Caucasian girls who seemed to have life without flaws or obstacles. We never really saw multiple sizes, shapes, or tones on the screen. As I got older and even today, the majority of beauties in the media are depicted as women who have a certain kind of hair, waistline, or butt shape.

Very rarely are we taught to embrace ourselves or receiving the message that it is okay being you. Even the men in society are seen flocking to a woman with a certain body type instead of promoting those women who are being themselves. Absolutely no shade to any woman who does what's needed to embrace her looks or body. As I do things that make me feel excited about myself: hair, makeup, exercise, and weight loss techniques; my view is that there are no "absolutes" when it comes to beauty, we are all beautiful in our own right.

"I'm beautiful." I can't tell you how good it feels to say that. That is something I, at one time, wasn't able to say. Even after I lost weight and fought to get my weight together, I still struggled with believing I was beautiful at times. How are you showing you that you love you? It was time for me to do some more work in my process. The funny thing is, it will take constant effort to show appreciation to yourself. It is of the utmost importance to recognize your power within. To identify with the, "you," inside. I so love myself. Sometimes I just look at myself and say, "Girl you are the bomb." Because I am. I'm a loving person and I care for people.

As I've been able to discover my beauty, I've devoted my life to show others what I know, what I have experienced, and what has worked for me. I completely understand that broken girl, that damaged girl, the girl that gives more to others than she gives to herself, and the girl falling short in many things because she never feels valued. I even know the girl who doesn't know what she loves about herself or what she is worthy of. Girl look, I understand you, and I can help you. I actually want to help you. Finding the beauty in myself means that I'm still discovering, still working, and still learning. But with every lesson I learn, I'm always willing to share, mainly because as I help you, I'm still helping me sis.

WHAT DO YOU SEE IN THE MIRROR?

BY MELISSA LYNN

"What do you see when you look in the mirror?" After a long pause, I respond, tired eyes, I have been traveling so much lately. But I also see a determined woman embracing the opportunity to rediscover who she is. Then another glance in the mirror, I see a forty-year-old woman welcoming the next chapter of her life. She is single for the first time since high school, stepping into her soul's calling, and opening her own coaching business. I see a woman sharing herself with you here, naked, raw, authentic, and unafraid. Let's be clear, not naked in the sense of no clothing, but naked as in stripping off the masks that would hide my true self from all of you. I can honestly say that I am comfortable for the first time in my own skin.

Let me start by saying that I have not always been comfortable showing vulnerability publicly. As many of you know, vulnerability is the core of shame, fear, and unworthiness. Fear of judgment and lack of self-worth has plagued my thoughts for years. My fear was backed with an infinite cycle of shame amassing evidence to confirm why I wasn't worthy of _______ (insert desire). These thoughts were reinforced by continued stories repeated over and over throughout my childhood and adult life—either as my own repetitious thoughts to myself or as stories I heard from others around me. Some of the more significant stories that have had the most impact on my decisions were: 1) Stewart (biological father) chose to sign over his parental rights to stop his obligation for child support. Apparently, he had better things to do than raise children. 2) Stewart had girlfriends in every city he went to. All of these women meant more to him than I did. 3) Too bad the big boob gene skipped right over you. 4) We live in New Mexico. You will always be taller than the boys. Get used to it. 5) That's what

I get for dating a white girl. 6) You have been on a diet since you were born. 7) To be more competitive you need to lose weight, ten pounds, preferably twelve. 8) Being heavy runs in the family. Finally, 9) You weigh more than____ (insert basically any boy my age). My developing mind at this age didn't see the difference between my 5'9" frame compared to the average 5'7" stature of the boys in my class.

These stories received even more validation through repeated patterns in my life. You have all heard the saying, "I have been dating the same man over and over with a different face," right? This had been my reality for years. I can remember dating a boy in high school who, while on a date with me, started kissing another girl. In that moment of confusion and devastation, all I could think was, "What is wrong with me?" These thoughts quickly turned into a multitude of negative self-talk and dishonoring affirmations that reinforced the stories defining my life. The pattern continued with me throughout my first marriage. I allowed the man who I had promised my love and future to, to disrespect me repeatedly for almost twelve years. Through all of the abuse (both physical and emotional) and all the other women, I was unable to see my value and honor my true spirit. I allowed the opinions of those closest to me to define my worth. I also let the chatter and opinions of even my closest supporters to influence my decision thus allowing the cycle of abuse to repeat.

Still holding the mirror in my hands, I take another look. I believe the universe has a way of bringing people into our lives for a purpose. There are life lessons in every interaction we encounter. I also believe that not everyone is supposed to stay in our lives forever. It took a long time for me to accept that relationships, not just romantic ones, can have an expiration date. People come and go, and it is important to remember that we need to look for the lessons and be thankful for every opportunity to grow.

Having finally lost all the baby weight I gained while pregnant with my two children, I started to feel a subtle shift in my spirit. I subconsciously called forth the man who would become my second husband. It wasn't until much later that I learned this "calling" was from a confused state. After all, how could I possibly find true love when I was riddled with insecurities, doubting my every decision, and had little to no self-worth? The man in which I thought was my soul mate turned out to be a mirrored reflection of all my past wounds

I left untreated. Remember, feelings buried alive don't die. Instead they smolder until they resurface at a time or in a manner we cannot control and are almost always unpleasant! I was in my late twenties, had just finished college, and had a wonderful man who placed me on a pedestal. What more could a girl ask for, right? Through this twelve-year period of my life, we started two businesses. One did extremely well while the other failed miserably. Many decisions were made that I was not comfortable with; however, I felt my opinion was unvalued therefore I stopped speaking my mind. Essentially, I just rolled with the flow. Heck, at the end of the day, I was living in a beautiful house in one of the most desirable neighborhoods, finally driving the Mercedes of my dreams, in Las Vegas partying and shopping the weekends away, and all I had to do was continue to bury my feelings and silence my voice. I can tell you that at this time I was ill-equipped to deal with the stress and anxiety that came with being a business owner. There were many months that it was feast or famine. In addition to the entrepreneur life, I was dealing with the ups and downs of co-parenting with my ex while simultaneously trying to blend my family with my new husband's. Needless to say, I found solace in food. Lots and lots of food! Over the course of three years, I gained over one hundred pounds. I was so embarrassed and ashamed of what my life had become. I hated myself and my appearance. I could not stand to look at myself in the mirror. My self-talk at this point was devastating. I was literally living in two pairs of jeans because I refused to spend any money on clothes to fit this body that I hated so much when I had closets full of designer clothes I could no longer wear. Thank goodness I was able to wear my husband's clothes during this time. But then again, this was only a crutch that allowed me to continue my destructive behavior. As the business continued to flourish, so did my weight. Quickly, I realized that money truly cannot buy you happiness. There is no dollar amount that will fix what is hurting inside.

I have been asked many times what my breaking point was. I honestly believe it came after seeing a photo of myself from my niece's wedding. Who was this woman? I didn't even recognize myself in the picture. Who was this person sitting next to my children? She was so sad, depressed, and unhappy. She was ME! I cried off and on for several days. I couldn't believe how much weight I allowed myself to gain. I was angry at myself for becoming so unhealthy and jeopardizing the most important person in my children's lives: me. I was completely judgmental and hateful to myself. There is no way I would have had any friends if I spoke to others in the same manner that I spoke to myself.

Then the day came when I pulled myself up off the couch and powered on my treadmill. I just started walking. I was completely out of breath after just fifteen minutes. The athlete I once was no longer existed, but I was determined to keep walking. Fifteen minutes turned into thirty, then forty, sixty, and so on. I can recall nights when I was walking on the treadmill desperately trying to complete my workout while my family sat on the couch in front of me eating ice cream and popcorn while watching movies. I felt so alone and had very little support from those around me. This frustration turned into motivation and pushed me harder. I learned that the support I was searching for was already there; it was inside myself. As I started releasing the weight, I decided to learn more about food and how to properly nourish my body. Eating fast food/gas station hot dogs became a thing of the past. The biggest lesson for me was learning proper portion sizes. I took back the control of my body, food, and my physical activity. My walking over time became jogging, then running. I discovered that there was, in fact, such a thing as “runners high,” and it was amazing! By this time, I was down approximately ninety pounds, and seeing the results of my efforts kept me going. I was determined to reach the -100 club, and I DID! I learned that I am very goal oriented. I needed the next “thing” to chase. This is when I decided to train for my first half marathon. To go from being extremely overweight, yes I’m going to say it, OBESE, to a runner was a huge accomplishment. I set my sights on the Nike Women's Half Marathon in San Francisco. This is the race known for rewarding its participants with a Tiffany’s necklace at the finish line all wrapped up in the signature Tiffany blue box and delivered by way of a fireman in tuxedo. I couldn’t think of a better way to celebrate myself and all my hard work than to participate in such an exciting event.

My training (running) became an obsession for me. I didn’t understand this at the time, but running gave me the opportunity to occupy my mind and bury the feelings of hurt and betrayal I was feeling in my marriage. The old me would have turned to food in an effort to console myself. The new and what I thought of as improved version of myself just kept running. Soon after the successful completion of the half marathon, I found myself dealing with yet another affair. How could he do this to me again? What does he see in her that I don't have? I just didn't understand. I dedicated myself to being his personal cheerleader and always supporting his needs before my own. Just like that, all of the negative self-talk and lack of self-worth flooded my mind once more. It didn't matter that I was now down one hundred and fifteen pounds and more fit than I have ever been. I wasn't good enough for him. I remember standing in the mirror and all I could see was the loose skin, the stretch marks, the bags under my eyes from lack of sleep and puffiness from crying. My inner critic refused to see the slim, strong, muscular 5'9" reflection staring back at me.

About this time my dear friend introduced me to one of my first mentors in personal growth/self-development work. What I was hearing resonated instantly with my soul, and the awakening began. I spent hours reading, listening to podcasts, and attending live events. I was eager to learn and couldn't get enough. I dove into the process with an open mind, but more importantly, an open heart. I allowed myself the time and needed space to process my thoughts and feelings. I invested in my own coaches and therapists for support, and embraced the tools and techniques they offered to better handle the blocks that were holding me back. I was introduced to the concept of the "when/then" cycle I had been stuck in my entire life. You know, the WHEN I lose the last ten pounds THEN I will be______. WHEN I meet the perfect guy THEN I will be_____. WHEN I get this job THEN I will be______. Once I learned that these moments I was chasing would never actually bring the happiness and freedom I was seeking, my life changed forever. I have learned how to forgive myself for past decisions, actions, and behaviors that I have been ashamed of for far too long, and I no longer hold judgment or resentment in my heart for them. I will no longer allow my future to pay for the experiences of my past.

As I pick the mirror up from my lap and look at myself once more, I say, "I know that I am not broken, I am whole and complete just as I am. I know that my lack of confidence and unhappiness was never truly about my weight or my outward appearance. For me, finding the beauty inside came from learning to love all of me, all of my "imperfections." And I say imperfection lightly because the majority of what we view as inadequate comes from what others (society) project onto us as “worthiness” or “enough.” When I say all of me, I am referring to not just the physical, my loose skin, stretch marks, my long toes, wrinkles, and my weight, but also my stories, my life lessons, my decisions, and my experiences. I understand now that ALL of these parts make me the strong, confident, empowered woman sitting before you today. For her, I am thankful and truly BLESSED!

MY BODY LED ME TO MY HEART

BY MICHELLE TORRES

What is your heart telling you? Huge question, tough answers. First let me start by saying that by trade I am a nurse. I've been a registered nurse for twelve years, worked in many specialties, mostly pediatrics, and currently nurse case management and administration. So when it comes to the heart, I do know a thing or two about it, its function, and anatomy. But I can tell you without reservation that the physical part of your heart is not the most important part. I've struggled my entire life in this constant battle between my heart and my mind: my mind telling me one thing and my heart telling me another. Somewhere in between this constant struggle has been my body. I think my body struggle ultimately led me back to my heart.

Growing up, I had an amazing childhood. My parents are the kind of people who created a life that most people could only dream about. Not that we always had the fanciest and best cars, houses, and things, but they created a home full of the most tangible love. We had fun hanging out at home together. Summers spent traveling to new and fun places with family and friends—always a new adventure. Christmas mornings full of surprises and joy—every holiday like that, really. My parents taught me to be strong, independent, honest, loyal, and kind. I grew up into the fierce woman I am today, and I will forever be thankful that their love helped mold and shape me into the person I am. I was truly loved and accepted for who I was for just being myself, and I never remember a time when they weren't there. The more people I meet who never had that kind of love and support, the more I realize how truly fortunate I was to have had that kind of environment to grow up in.

So what struggle could this fiercely independent woman I'm describing possibly have, you might ask? Well, the answer is that constant struggle of body image. I was taught that spirit and heart triumph above all, but when I was growing up, I found out quickly that there is always some dark tangible force that wants to objectify and degrade a woman until she is nothing but an object of desire, a sex toy, someone to use and throw out like last month's magazine issue. Don't even get me started on magazines and the unrealistic expectations the advertisement industry sets on GIRLS, I mean young girls, and women.

I blossomed very young; apparently my womanly curves started to show right around sixth grade. I had hips, breasts, and "the body of a woman," as one of my girlfriends I ran into a few years back told me. I ran into this, now, woman I had not seen in years, who was herself a newly blessed momma, pushing her infant son around at a store. I think I told her she looked the same and congratulated her on her little new addition. She told me that I looked the same too, and I probably said something self-degrading, and then what she said next shocked me. She told me, "You REALLY look the same because you had the body of a woman when we were in like sixth grade. I hated you!" I don't know why, but in that moment all the key pins in the lock of a

National Treasurer/Indiana Jones/Tomb Raider type movie clicked into place and the lock turned. I understood why I had such a hard time with my female friends growing up. I remembered the conflicts I had with most, not all, of my girlfriends growing up, and I was always left with this empty feeling of not understanding why. A lot of things made sense now.

But why did it have to be that way? I needed those relationships with those girlfriends during that time the most. I gave up on women and developed more friendships with boys. They were easier, less emotional, liked to just have fun, and I felt appreciated for my spunk and my heart—my mind more than my behind, which worked great for me because that is how I was raised. Or so I thought. I wonder how many of those boys would have been my friends if I were more Ugly Betty than Betty Page. Not that I am saying I am the most beautiful woman on the planet because, by far, I know I am not. However, I'm sure my tiny waist (at the time) and huge boobs didn't hurt my prospects, which brings me to the subject of male attention. I didn't realize it at the time, but I apparently drew a lot of male attention. I always had these little dates and boyfriends very young. I remember this 27-year-old guy asking me for my number, because girls that's how it worked back then, and I was thirteen years old! Thirteen! I was way too young to be dating. I was still a baby, had no idea what I wanted in life, but I always had a boyfriend. I really don't know if any of them really loved me for me. It wasn't my parents' fault or my fault that all this happened, that God gave me a body, but I thank God every day he gave me a mind and a heart too.

Growing up with all these images of what a woman should look like, magazines, movies, whatever—I never truly saw myself as beautiful. I was never and could never be as beautiful as "those" girls, so I focused on who I was and who I wanted to be. I also sacrificed myself a lot to fit in and be accepted by others, and I never realized that if I was 100% myself maybe those people would accept me for who I really was inside. Even my ex-husband of nine years I don't think ever truly appreciated me for the person I am inside, for my heart, although I'm sure he appreciated all of my outside physical...ahem...assets. Now I fight to be my authentic self always; whether or not people like it is more irrelevant now. I think that if they don't accept me for who I am, they were never truly meant to be "my" people.

Many people don't know this about me, but because I was young and rebellious and always had a lot of "friends" I got myself into a lot of trouble and was a high school dropout. In developing and sacrificing myself, I tried to be the "cool" girl. I spent a couple of years not pursuing what I truly wanted and not feeding my heart, until I finally had a huge breaking point. This is when God found me and brought me back and I started once again to listen to my heart. This brings me to my first question, "What is your heart telling you?" and this brings up one more question: "What does your heart really want?" So bear with me because I'm going to put on my nursing hat and tell you some things about your heart. Trust me, it is relevant.

Your heart is an organ that fuels your entire body. Its anatomy includes four chambers, two atria (small chambers on top), two ventricles (large chambers on bottom), and multiple arteries. The way the heart works is that the valves between the chambers open and close to allow blood to flow into and out of the chambers of the heart. The heart muscle contracts to push blood out of the heart and relaxes to also allow blood to fill the chambers. The atria (small top chambers) fill with blood first, then when the mitral and tricuspid valves open the blood then fills the larger bottom chambers, the ventricles: right atrium to right ventricle and left atrium to left ventricle. The left side of the heart pushes oxygenated blood out to the entire body via the aorta, and the right side of the heart received the deoxygenated blood from the body and pushes it to the lungs to pick up oxygen. The heart also has a plexus of arteries around it that give it its very own supply of oxygen-rich blood and takes the deoxygenated blood away from the heart itself.

Now that you've had your anatomy lesson, there is a little-known fact about the heart, outside of the medical community of course, and that is that it has one artery in the above-mentioned plexus with a serious, vital function. This artery looks like all the rest and is structurally the same in design but not in purpose. This is the left anterior descending artery (LAD). This artery supplies blood to almost the entire left side of the heart...to get technical, the anterolateral myocardium, apex, and intraventricular septum. In plain English, the front and bottom (apex) of the left ventricle and the front of the area that divides the bottom of the heart.

"Why is this important?" "Who cares!?!" Bear with me again. Many people don't know that this one little artery can affect your life in just minutes. A heart attack resulting from a complete or almost complete LAD blockage will cause death 88% of the time outside of the hospital setting. This type of heart attack is often referred to as the "widow maker." This question is, "Why would this one little artery be so vital?" Answer in two parts: (1) This artery is responsible for supplying blood to the actual heart muscle. The heart muscle needs this oxygen-rich blood supply to have everything it needs to perform its job, to contract and push blood out of the heart. (2) Why would an artery that supplies less than 50% of the heart muscle blood supply be so important? Second part of the answer is because the left side of the heart pushes out all the oxygen-rich blood out to the rest of the body. It literally breathes life to the entire body and in turn itself. Crazy huh!?! If the body isn't getting all of the oxygen to all of the tissues everything starts to die, but the first thing to start dying is the heart itself.

Why does this matter? Why did you take me on this anatomical journey? I hated science after all, you say. What does this have to do with me? Quick answer. My body journey has taught me that what you don't give life to in your life dies, especially your heart. If your heart dies, every part of your body will die. I believe the same is true for your spiritual heart, your inner-self heart, however you see your "heart" figuratively. I am a spiritual person, so I see this as truth when I read God's Word, the Bible (going there). *"Guard your heart with all diligence, for out of it is the wellspring of life"* (Proverbs 4:23). For me this is guarding my heart from the lies of the world that say, "You aren't pretty enough," "skinny enough," "capable enough," "young enough," "smart enough" to make your dreams come true, or "You don't deserve the things you want, you'll never get them." Not one of these lies is true, and I am tired of the lies that try to reinforce that they are.

I would take it further to say what you don't feed dies. So what are you feeding your heart? Are you listening to it? What is it saying? What does it want? Only you can answer these questions for yourself. When is the last time you truly listened to your heart?

There are five (5) aspects of health that I believe affect your heart: mental health, emotional health, physical health, social health, and spiritual health. I think we have to feed our hearts in each one of these areas to be whole and complete. The older I get, the more I know that my social health needs those strong women relationships that I so desperately needed in my younger years. Not that I am not still friends with men, but the lines are definitely different. I make it a practice to try to do things that feed my health in these areas, at least one daily, and take time to stop and listen to my heart weekly.

For me, I think my heart wants me to love and accept myself as the person God created me to be, to love my true self. The inner child, wondrous and pure, the full grown adult woman, fierce and strong, a warrior—and whatever your religious preference or background, I believe it is true for you too! God called Gideon when he was in hiding from a warring nation, Midian, threshing wheat in secret. *"The angel of the Lord appeared to him and said to him. 'The Lord is with you, mighty warrior!'"* (Judges 6:12). God called him while he was hiding in fear. God does not see you the way you see you. His ways are not our ways, and His thoughts are not our thoughts. I am always comforted and astounded by God's love for me, for all of us really, and the many ways He has blessed me and given me unique gifts to give back to the world.

And for me, the things that feed my heart are being around my family and the people I love and chilling with my perfect dog...yes, I'm completely biased. I love spending time at church and serving in whatever capacity God leads me. I love lightning and fireworks, the smell of the desert when it rains, the cool mountain air. I love flowers, campfires, and cowboy boots, and will never apologize for being me.

This is the best advice I could give, but really it's something I need to tell myself, and that is "Beautiful girl, you only have one life to live, live it on your terms, with your unique style and gifts. Feed your heart, don't let it die. There is only one unique you. Be your authentic self. Live your authentic life. 'Your' people will come join you on your journey, and the right ones will stay."

I AM NOT MY BODY; I AM MORE THAN THAT

BY MICHELLE PAUL

Age nine is the first time I remembered really hearing, "You are pretty." However, it was in comparison to my female siblings. I am not sure how I felt about that statement. As a matter of fact, it did not make me feel. It just made me wonder why they would say such a thing. At that time, I had just moved from Trinidad and Tobago to America with my mother, stepfather, and three siblings I did not grow up with. The transition was difficult; I went from being the only child to being child number three chronologically.

Junior high is when I first realized that my body weight, size, and shape didn't look like that of my sisters and female friends. My body did not get the attention of the boys. This same pattern played out in high school. Even as an adult, my mindset was, *I will never get the attention of the men*. Again, my body failed me. I remember the struggle to find clothes and shoes. I was fat and had to shop for the bigger sizes. At age fourteen, I was wearing size 17 clothing and size 11 and on to size 12 shoes by the end of high school. Even as a child, finding age-appropriate shoes was a challenge. I remember we went from store to store looking, and I would end up with an adult size. As I write this, I realize that prior to coming to America all of my clothes were custom-made by a seamstress or tailor. I had lots of clothes. I remember my dresses hanging in the wardrobe neatly hung. It seems like I was measured monthly for a new outfit for church or special events. School clothes were never an issue because I wore a uniform every day until I moved to America.

As a young child, I experienced several bouts of molestation up until my early teens. I had the opportunity to work out my issues as a result of this type of abuse. Well, so I thought. As I struggle with my body image, I see clearly how being molested is a part of me loathing my body.

After high school, I gained more weight and was uncomfortable in my skin. I never really knew how to express what I felt about my body. What I did know is that the females I was around had smaller bodies and always got the attention of the males. I felt for sure that my body was unattractive and the reason that I was overlooked. I struggled with what I call "body envy" all of my life; however, I never gave it a voice until about five years ago. I always had negative thoughts about my body, my weight, and my height. I was always taller than my peers. So to make myself shorter I subconsciously started slouching my shoulders so I would seem smaller. As a result, I began to walk with a slouch. My slouchy walk and posture became my disapproval of myself. I was teased most of my junior and higher years. The American boys would make fun of me. They would mock/mimic my walk and call me Abdullah, who at that time was a huge slouch wrestler. I was so ashamed and would fear seeing these boys in the hallway; as I passed by them I would hang my head and arm myself for their ridicule of my slouchy walk and body. This time of shaming made me afraid and made me loathe my body and those American boys. This is the first time that I have shared this inner dialogue for which I have carried for thirty-eight years. In writing this, I just realized how much of an impact this experience has had on the distortion of my body that I carry in my mind.

As an adult, my body issues are a continuous plague to my mind and my experiences, especially in relationships with the opposite sex. As I'm thinking back on my feelings about my body, I possessed a mindset that reeked of self-judgments. I realize now why I kept my walls up and was gripped by fear for the one thing my soul desired: a relationship in which I felt accepted, loved, and wanted. However, my rejection of my body was in my way. I see now why I kept getting the things that kept me in this deep internal struggle with the size and shape of my body, particularly my belly. As the saying goes, "What you focus on grows," and my focus has been on wanting a body that I think would be attractive and that the opposite sex would desire. What I kept getting is everything to prove that my body is unattractive and undesired by a man.

In 2008, I decided to have weight loss surgery (gastric bypass). I would lose a total of

120 pounds. My lowest weight was 173, down from 292. For a moment, I wore a size 10. However, my mind never made the connection because I did not recognize myself in that body. I then stabilized at a size 12, and my mind still did not make the connection. Physically I was a size 12 and psychologically I remained a size 22. Yes, I received the compliments on how nice I looked, comments like "keep that size" and "do not gain back that weight." So in my mind I was right, my body was a failure. So imagine the fear that gripped my soul when I began to gain the weight back. I would look in the full-length mirror and be horrified. I felt powerless and hopeless. I hated my body, especially my belly fat. I struggled with what I call "belly envy." I swear I hated my belly fat. I would look at everyone's belly, and I would envy the women with flat bellies. I remember my girlfriend at the time telling me to stop complaining about my belly fat. She would say, paraphrasing, "Your belly is not that big." However, for me my belly is a big monster. That part of my

body was disgusting, just hideous. Then there was my back fat and big arms; the battle ensued. Yes, the struggle is real. Imagine, I brought this way of thinking to my relationships with the men I had dated. I would be out with a man and feel totally insecure. My self-talk was locked on telling me that he wanted every other woman that was smaller because they were sexy, unlike me. In my mind I would question why he was with me. I never felt like I was there with them because mentally I was on trial in my head and the sound of the calved hitting the bench was loud. My last relationship was the first time I ever felt secure, and that was because I did enough work on my mindset to believe what he said he saw about me—which was my height and my size—and he was immediately attracted. For the first time in my life, I felt in my skin, I felt secure, and I experienced feeling sexy. I was free. I didn't have to hide. Having sex was liberating. I finally felt what it was like to embody my body, and I wasn't on trial in my head. I was in the moment and enjoying the pleasure of having sex and being fully in a relationship. As things in this relationship began to go south, I experienced more weight gain, and the trial judge in my head started back. Now, I was verbal with my feelings about my body. Even with reassurance from my partner, I totally relapsed. In the last year, I have started to begin the journey of accepting my body. After a conversation with my sister, she sent me a song. She said, "I heard this song and I immediately thought about you." As I listened, I cried and cried. I would listen to that song every day over and over for months. This song by Jessi J, "QUEEN," re-engaged my thoughts about emancipating my mind and accepting my body. For me, acceptance means love. I am not where I desire to be, however, I am far away from where I was, and for me that means prudence. I am growing, and I am moving in the direction of full acceptance of fully loving my body.

My test of this came in June and September of 2018. In June, I decided to join the Naked and Unafraid Book Anthology, and in September I attend the Naked and Unafraid Retreat and Book Collaboration. This retreat was an amazing, liberating, and freeing weekend. I would meet thirteen remarkable women of whom I knew nothing about. We shared our stories, and we psychologically and physiologically got naked together. I came to the retreat open to meeting new people and with the yearning to use my mind and emotions in a different way. Boy, did I get what

I desired. Our retreat package included a photo shoot and a spa treatment. We were encouraged and not pressured to do the naked photo shoot. I gave it some thought and over time decided I was not ready to see my belly fat in pictures, so I opted to wear something sexy (see pic at end). During this time together, we chose two foundation words; the first day my word was “Gratitude,” and the second day my word was “Forgiven.” As I uncovered, unpacked, and reframed my mindset on a relationship issue I was struggling with for almost two years, I felt light from the support and feedback I received from the women. I was in an amazing space. Then it was Spa Day. I remember hearing that we would need to be naked and put on the clothes (requirement) we would receive from the spa. I was good. Upon arrival, we checked in, dropped off our shoes, and picked up our spa clothing. Now, what I thought I heard turned into having to be totally naked, meaning I had to take off all of my clothes in front of my new women friends and all the other women who were in the locker room and spa area. Needless to say, my mind went into an emotional Chinese fire drill. For a couple of seconds, I did not breathe and wanted to STOP and SIT it out. I told the women that I would need some trauma work if I were to go naked. All of my emotions, self-talk, and talking out loud lasted for about two minutes. I just couldn't bring myself to do it. Then I heard my inner voice say, "You have to do it, so figure it out." I stopped for a while to figure out how I would walk from the lockers to the spa area naked. I paced around for a moment and finally, I found the spa's towels. Of course, they were the size of hand towels, so I figured I would need to take two of them to cover up my belly fat. Yes, I took all of my clothes off and proceeded to cover up with the two hand towels and made my way into the spa shower area. I am still in disbelief that I am doing the naked thing. I managed to take the shower naked, and then I made my way to one of the ten spas covered with the towels I intercepted in the locker room. I entered one of the spa tubs and placed the towels on the side. Again, my self-talk was in motion. I heard, "Michelle this is your body, nothing is going to change right now, so just accept it and be naked." So, I did. I just focused on accepting that this moment is all there is, and I was naked in it. As I slowly suspended my judgment of my nakedness, I eased into it with ease. In the spa with my women friends, my other foundation word was forgiven. At that moment, I was in full GRATITUDE for the courage I exuded for feeling FORGIVEN from the loathing of my body.

As I reflect back on my retreat experiences, I realize my need to be brutally honest with myself. As I begin to check in with myself, I discovered that I am out of control with my eating and I feel empty. I now want to take a deep look at what those feelings are about because I know it is my reason for overeating and creating a body that is unhealthy and unaccepted by me. So I made the decision to find a therapist to begin my work. What I know for sure is that I need to continue doing the inner work of digging deeper into myself because I want to be authentically full of gratitude for this body of mine. I love this quote: "Gratitude unlocks the fullness of life. It turns what we have into enough and more. It turns denial into acceptance, chaos to order, confusion to clarity. It can turn a meal into a feast, a house into a home, a stranger to a friend," (Melody Beattie). Choosing the foundation word "GRATITUDE" was no accident; it was divinely orchestrated just for me. After leaving the retreat, I take a moment each day to have gratitude for my body and how it is serving me. As my journey of becoming body-confident unfolds, I am willing to dig deeper into myself and am allowing gratitude to be my way of life. I am open to the fullness of my life, the feelings of being more than enough, gaining more clarity about myself, and accepting—that is, loving this significant, magnificent, awesome body of mine. This freedom I am after is not for a man or anyone else to accept or validate my body; it for me to accept my body as it is and do the work for me to create the body I so desire. My NAKED and UNAFRAID experience was a divine setup for me to begin the journey of accepting that I am not my body; I am more than that! Namaste!

TWO STRIKES!

BY NATALIE BRYAN

I struggled a lot with the whole idea of writing a chapter in a book about body confidence! In my mind, I was laughing. Me? Body confidence, whew! As a child and just social individual in a world where we are all looking to be loved and accepted, it was sad that I always heard two things growing up. You have two strikes against you: You're fat and you're black. Wow, what a thought, right? What a concept! How do you process that as a child in today's society? What can that do to your self-esteem? What does that actually do to your self-esteem? Just letting you know today, this day I am a plus-size queen!

Throughout my early years in life growing up in a West Indian home and surrounded by my culture, being chubbier or "healthier" was so widely accepted. I loved going to Jamaica. You would always see pictures of a very skinny man with a very heavy, "healthy" lady. He would be chasing after her on a bike or walking her down the street. Those memories still bring a smile to my face. What I loved most were the unadulterated expression of love and how he would adore her so much! I would hear certain terms of endearment like "chubby," "maumpi," "biggas," or "fatty bum bum"! Surprisingly, it was not meant to be disrespectful or have a negative connotation. My parents, both Jamaicans, separated early on in my life; however, my mother always made sure that we were very aware of where we came from. Traveling often as a child to Jamaica, I would love to hear cousin Angela, a plus-size queen herself, tell the story of when I was six months old and my asthma was so bad that she had to take me to Jubilee Hospital and she would be so animated saying, "Mek sure unnu tek care a har a foreign shi cum from" (Make sure you take care of her; she's from America)! I felt sure and secure with my weight in that culture and in that space. Up until just a few years ago, I would still say, "I can't wear that outfit here in the U.S. but wait until I get home (Jamaica) and I am rocking it."

Although I remember being heavier than most of the other children, it was so surprising to me that as I look back at pictures of myself when I was younger, I wasn't fat; I was thicker than most of the other children and solid, but I wasn't fat. I didn't realize until later in life that those many nights in the hospital, sometimes weeks at a time, that it was the steroids because of my severe asthma. I remember being alone in a hospital bed with plastic draped around my head pushing oxygen into my lungs, just wanting to play like other kids. People think that they know your story and create these narratives that if we are not careful it can become your narrative.

I have come to realize how people's words cannot only hurt but derail visions, hopes, self-esteem, and dreams. Boy, when the Bible says speak those things as though they were, for death and life is in the tongue! It really is the truth! Two strikes! I was already at a deficit, and to make it worse, I was the first child! I honestly say that it has not been easy for me being the first child of a first-generation immigrant household in the U.S. The whole dynamic of straddling two cultures is a whole different story for another day, but to say I was looking for acceptance and love from everyone, including family, is an understatement.

You want to fit in with your peers, and school was a real struggle for me. Although life growing up wasn't bad, things were tight. We grew up in a middle-class family, and although we had some nice things, I didn't have name-brand clothes or shoes, and to be honest with you I didn't even realize there was a difference until JHS. I was here just trying to balance being Jamaican-American. I didn't always get my hair done, and I would always compare myself to others. I remember elementary school going into junior high school feeling so out of place. I remember trying to emulate others, not really sure of who I was; sadly, this phase lasted way longer than I care to admit. I was bullied a lot. I was called fat and black! Where did I remember hearing those words? Oh yeah! I have two strikes against me. Why didn't I stand up for myself? Where was my voice? I was quiet, and I was quiet because in my household you are taught that children were to be seen and not heard.

I am not sure when all the negative words actually set in my spirit or even when it began to take root; however, they eventually began to manifest. I believed all of it. I could only hear Fat and Black in my mind for a very long time.

As I grew older, I noticed older men appreciating my body more than they should! I was young and being approached by men in their twenties and thirties, and I was still in my mid-teens. Although that should make people feel empowered, it made me initially feel insecure. But then you know what happens when one seeks love and acceptance. I started to focus on my body, accentuating what I had, presenting it as more mature. The fact that I had thicker thighs and bigger breast did nothing to help.

It was in high school that I believe I first started seeing glimmers of my body confidence.

I no longer cared about how people thought of me. I had a new set of people that encouraged me and accepted me for who I was, and that placed me in a better position to start loving myself more. It is amazing what words of kindness, genuine emotion, and affection can do to someone in such a short period of time. It's crazy looking back at how I was so enamored with what people thought about me!

I didn't think about the amazing things that I was doing in my life, what my mother was exposing me to, and what I was learning. At that time, my mother had several businesses, and I was right at her side. I was doing major things, having business encounters and exchanges. I was learning how to make money very early. I was dealing with banks, companies, and manufacturers. When teens just had things like dating and partying to think about, I was running businesses. I didn't have the luxury of thinking about the next name brand or where the next party was going to be held.

Those experiences carved me into the woman that I am now. Now when I said I saw glimmers of body confidence in high school that does not mean that I was out here like, "Oh, I'm the best thing since sliced bread." I still had a lot of insecurities. You remember my two strikes, right? I originally resented being dark-skinned and being in this body because I felt that there was something always inherently wrong with me, because that's what I was told. My faith and the development of a relationship with God empowered me and took away some of my insecurities. In the church, you always heard you were fearfully and wonderfully made and how much God loves you. As that relationship grew, so did the relationship with who I was. It wasn't that I still didn't have some insecurities or fear, but I felt that someone had my back unconditionally. I am thankful for a praying grandmother and her introducing me to Christ as a child because I spent many years talking to him about my fears, my dreams, my hurts, and my accomplishments.

This skin I am in doesn't define who I am as a person. It is just a piece of me, a part of who I am. As I began to educate myself about not only God but also about my culture, my African and Cuban origins, I saw beauty on a whole different level. I saw how beauty standards varied from culture to culture and how dark skin is beautiful, how fuller bodies were envied, and how societies pressured women to conform to their cultures. Honestly, if I were a blind person, I would think that being plus-sized was a curse considering how it's described in this culture. Even when given a compliment, it's mostly given with a negative connotation. "You're so pretty for a dark-skinned girl" or "You a big girl, but you cute!" There are so many stigmas about being plus size that it saddens me. "Beauty is in the eye of the beholder." That quote resonates with me because my beauty transcends this body.

As I am getting older I will be working on myself daily, making sure that whatever size I am, I am happy, healthy, and still have another pitch at a home run!

ROUGHLY FOR THE MOMENT: A TESTIMONY OF GOD'S FAITHFUL LOVE

BY PATRICIA COOK

Since being born, I've always loved God and openly had a foundation rooted in having Him in my life. My name is Patricia Cook. In 1975, I was born in New Orleans, LA, where our culture is surrounded by good food and music. Presently, I live in Moody, AL, which is twenty-five minutes from Birmingham, AL. Wait a minute! From teaching English and creative writing, I've accepted it to be true that I need an exciting opening. Since this is my first book contribution, I'm thinking, why can't I start off with a pun related to Body

Talk? So, I've just got to start off my chapter with my favorite pun about myself, which includes some foreshadowing for what you're about to read about my life, roughly over the last five and a half months. In fact, here it goes:

My maiden name is Patricia Marilyn Flotte. Thirteen years ago, I married a man with the last name Cook; do you see where I'm headed? Luckily, it wasn't something like the last name of Smith; then I'd be Patricia Marilyn Smith, known as "P.M.S.," and I'd live in Moody. This would seem about appropriate. HA! Please give me some leniency; this is my first book, and I have written mainly poetry over the last six years. Anyway, I grew up Presbyterian, became a Baptist, and now attend a non-denominational church called The Church of Highlands. I get this out-of-the-box thinking, strong-willed characteristic plainly outright and here's how: I've grown up with a learning disability called CAPD (Central Auditory Processing Disorder) with characteristics of dyslexia, dyscalculia, and dysgraphia; been a part of alternative ways of teaching methods and pedagogies such as Montessori and Orton-Gillingham for the past fifteen years; and don't forget I'm from New Orleans...Need I Say

More! I do have to say, I have only gotten to know Jesus more since I married a Baptist in 2005.

Internally, in my head as I'm writing I'm thinking two things about my chapter: 1) Is this going to be a chapter like I've always wanted to do or a short story? 2) Is it my testimony or God's testimony to myself that I am writing? Because for the past five and a half months, God has been speaking and showing His love for me in ways he had never done before. You might ask yourself, did you audibly hear Him? No, He has spoken to me through the Bible verses that I've read, through people that I've come into contact with, and through all my everyday on-goings. Has this ever happened to you too and do you think that it could? He has spoken to me in ways that I'd only have read about or had dreamed of happening to me. I wanted to tell you right off the bat: the first verse He presented to me five and a half months ago was Hebrews 4:16. In this verse, God says, "*Let us then approach God's throne of grace with confidence, so that we may receive* ***mercy*** *and find* ***grace*** *to help us in the time of need.*" I received this message from God on December 28, 2017 from the YouVersion Bible App. Please note: As you read my story, you will see an underlying theme in the last five and a half months and for my life. I will not spoil the underlying themes; however, this verse has two out of the four for which I will uncover as I write and you read this testimony!! This has been a rough five and a half months in more ways than one way for this Southern lady (as my close friends know, I'm saying this with a grain of salt). **So the story begins...**

The Cusp

It was December 28, 2017 at my family's beautiful beach house on the white, clear-crystal sands of West Beach in Gulf Shores, AL. It is in the last few days over the Christmas Break for which I break from teaching/tutoring, with daughter and husband out of school and work. Here's the setting of this crucial day and pivotal point in my life: I was sitting on the couch looking at my phone and my husband was at the round, glass dinner table working on his computer with Ladybug, our dog, on the floor between my husband and myself. I get up from the couch and say to my husband, let's pray for our **reconciliation** and that I had prayed all night for this (see The Highlands Christmas Online Sermon Archived for December 24th). We had been to The Grants Mill Reconciliation-themed sermon on Christmas Eve just four days before. I had only made this request to my husband because he seemed and acted agitated by myself and my family, since we had gotten to Gulf Shores on Christmas Day. I knew, based off of his short demeanor with myself mainly, that he was going through something majorly in his mind. I thought referencing this powerful Christmas sermon and implying for us to pray would open up his thoughts. And, so it DID! He said, "I have been thinking of us ending our marriage for good." Amongst other reasons, he said that he was not attracted to me anymore (I've put on twenty to thirty pounds since our marriage). He went on and on saying other reasons why and so on and so forth. In my mind, this was like the Trojan horse entering and attacking Troy, except it's his words and looks from his eyes attacking me. My mind was wandering in space and trying hard to grasp the concept of divorce. I could have gone on like we were forever the way we were, and I told him this. Also I had to agree about my weight being an issue (without telling him, of course); my weight was a size 12-14. I had always thought of myself as a "bigger" person. My dad was my idol, and he and I were a lot alike and everyone tells us so; he is a kind, good-hearted yet obese man. When I was ten years old, I wore a lady's size 10. In high school and college, I was bigger than my friends, which was roughly a size 8-10, and well you know...I never knew the BIGGER issue nor plan (excuse this pun). God has HIS plan for all of us!

Heavens

My best friend, her husband, and their three-year-old were due to arrive at the beach house one hour later after he left us at the beach to go back to Moody. My best friend had my back in any situation, and we've been best friends for twenty-seven years. When she gets there, I tell them the news and what had occurred just prior to them getting there. She was such a support for having been a child of divorce herself. That evening, I did not want to sit, relax, and hang out like we normally do, because if I sat I probably would have curled up in a ball and cried my eyes out. So, we sat in the kitchen on the countertops, talked, and did math problems all night, such as my weight contributed 90% (which is a good word for blamed) to the fact that a divorce was on my horizon, and 75% of this was to be blamed on my husband, and 25% on me. She did get a couple smiles out of me that night, especially after a while when another of our friends had arrived. Though, he did scare me with several of his mom's divorce stories. When it was time to go to bed and sleep, I cried all night long. My daughter was in the bed next to me; I was trying not to wake her with my wales and streaks of sobbing. I possibly got a whole hour of sleep that night.

The next morning, a rambunctious, sweet three-year-old was running around the house. Needless to say, we *Woke Up*! I then realized the other side of the bed was empty. I felt abandoned. Instantly, I snuggled with my most wonderful daughter. In her snuggle, I had the realization that I'm going to be a single parent. For possibly a year now, it's a good thing that I've worn a cross with a "diamond ring" around my neck that had represented that I'm married to God. Literally, I thought, *I'm married to God*, Yeah! Also, He'll take care of us!! The rest of the day is a blur. I did spend time with my parents. My mom said, "You've been abandoned," several times, and my dad cried, which I hadn't seen since his dad died in 1985. I love my parents so much and want to thank them for all the support!

The Cusp

It is now the cusp of the year 2017 ending and 2018 just beginning; the exact date is January 17, 2018 (I had literally gotten my own apartment four days after he left when only seeing it online). It is now 3 a.m.; I'm all alone on a "snowed-in" Wednesday morning in Moody, Alabama. Yes...I said, snowed-in. Alabama. Anyhow, the air is still, and the people in the neighboring apartments are inaudibly sleeping. Living in a hardworking, small, blue-collar town, I'm sure there are some people heating up their cars and getting ready for work. I have lived in Moody for the past thirteen years, but I have lived in these apartments roughly two weeks at this point. Mostly, the neighbors I've never met, except for some neighboring kids, the sweet apartment manager, and the two dark-colored ducks that appear to me as an odd-looking color. As I am writing, on this crisp and cold morning, I just made four cups of Community Coffee in order to consume as I check Facebook. Then, on Facebook, my good friend from five years prior had written, "I wish someone would walk with me at 6 a.m. for exercise." I wrote, "I wish I lived in Montgomery and I would." She in-boxed me and said, "I'm actually back in Moody and I live in some apartments." It turns out that her building is right across the street from mine in a rather large complex! What did God have instore for us!

When Life is But a Blink of the Eye

We walked and talked about three days a week for months and months. About two weeks into our sessions...I mean walks (HA!...did I mention my good friend is a life and job coach?), she told me about a RETREAT she was hosting in Dallas in September called Naked & Unafraid Women's Retreat Experience. Without hesitation, I was the first person to sign up. Months went by, I lost 25-30 pounds for which I did for myself (Promise: not a REVENGE BODY). It was now September 2018 and time for the retreat, and FYI, my husband and I ended up in counseling not divorce after almost having had signed the papers (literally seconds away). Still in drudgery of marriage counseling and my own personal spiritual work, I'm still living in the apartment; through Grace and Mercy, I'm working on and for myself meanwhile finding myself closer and closer to knowing God.

Still not knowing the BIGGER issue or plan, I was headed to Dallas on September 7th from Birmingham to Love Field Airport. When we got to the house of the retreat, I got a name tag with the special message of TRUTH typed into the top. In the first session, when the music stopped, we talked and had to write something positive about the other person on a paper attached to our backs. During this exercise someone asked, "What does TRUTH on your name tag mean to you?" I said, "I'm supposed to gain God's wisdom here. I think two times I've read this lately to pray for the wisdom of Jesus, and I'm just waiting for a third." During this exercise, others had written on my back that I was "friendly, brave and strong, patient and genuine" after only meeting me for a few minutes. I could agree instantly with these qualities (HA!). My good friend, who was my walking partner and hosting the retreat, always made me "look more at myself," to question my reaction to my husband leaving, and why this divorce almost happened. Never! Could I blame, in front of her, what happened with my husband on him. She wrote, "Tricia, I love your drive for wholeness. You are willing to do the work for yourself." Then, we had a day at the retreat that involved resting, professional pictures, and more self-help sessions. On that second night, in the last session for the day, we had to pick a card with a word on it, and mine said, "FAILURE." I was like: "What does this mean and why FAILURE? Why not love, warmth, hope (like others had pulled)? They were like, 'Good night.'" What this is, is my biggest insecurity related to being LD—nothing short of failure and the inability to please others! The next morning, we had another session before going to the all-day spa. The retreat facilitators handed out a sheet on the cycle of family dysfunction and on it listed behaviors based on characteristics and feelings related to dysfunction. At first, I would only identify with self-dependent, conflict-avoidance, victim, noble martyr, and self-righteousness (all being perceived by myself as the nicest). Then, I heard them say that the ones closest to us mirror what we are really like. Then, I had discovered that I really needed to look at the words that were left, and they were the not-so-nice ones but what I had seen in others closest to me. They are: controlling, victimizer, codependent behavior, and self-abandonment. Later on, inside the kiva of the spa, I was exploring "the darker side," the feelings and experiences associated with them. There in the kiva I had vision of Jesus come into my mind. He literally took away the pain and suffering and, in return, He gave me an open heart (LOVE). This shocked me, also not knowing that it is a precursor to the next morning (the last morning of the retreat).

I uncovered the TRUTH/Self-Abandonment=control and victimization along with the feeling of sadness, disappointment, and heartache due to failure in my past. This was what was behind ALL my problems with others; it really was me, not them! During the last session, which was a foot-washing, I had given my whole heart to JESUS. I felt SAVED for the first time, even though I had been through the rituals of becoming a Christian prior to this time. Nonetheless, I just don't just define myself as a Southern, Christian lady, teacher/tutor, educational consultant, ex-Girl Scout Leader and mom/wife who grew up thinking lesser of my relationship with God. Eventually, I had to look into my problems then into some issues of my childhood. I learned if you have problems with people, look into your issues. I felt like I had opened the door to Jesus but not entirely invited Him inside my heart until I had been placed in a situation of pain, struggle, and self-discovery. My message to you is: don't take things so seriously when Life is Rough-Rejoice in the GRACE, STRENGTH, FAITH, and LOVE of Jesus. Please take hold and meditate on the following scriptures related to my story:

Blameless Lives/Strength (Proverbs 20:7)

Grace/Truth (Ephesians 1:1-3)

Kimazing Photos

ABOUT THE AUTHORS

ALLISON DENISE ARNETT
Visionary Author

Meet Allison Denise, Book and Brand Designer and 2x Best-Selling Author. She has built her brand from the ground up using everything she's learned along the way. Fun facts: Allison is a degree accountant AND self-taught graphic designer with over 12 years in the industry. She's had the pleasure of designing beautiful boss brands and book covers for several speakers, authors, coaches, and creative writers over the last three and a half years as a full-time entrepreneur.

Allison Denise has a heart for women in business and finds joy in helping women influencers and authors increase their impact, influence, AND income by helping them design and launch beautiful books and brands. When she is not designing you can find her in Houston, TX loving on her three babies and being an advocate for self-love and self-acceptance via her Naked and Unafraid Women's Empowerment Movement. Learn more and connect with Allison Denise on her website www.branditbeautifully.com or on all social media @imallisondenise

JAMELLA STROUD
Visionary Author

Jamella Stroud, CEO and Founder of Naked & Unafraid Movement, is an international transformational speaker, author, and coach who values Jesus, family, community, and building relationships. After leaving her first career as a tax accountant to pursue her life's work and launched her second business Surge Coaching & Consulting. Jamella prides herself on her ability to bring a sudden, strong burst of energy, creativity, new ideas and thinking to her client interaction disturbing the norm, and status quo, pushing boundaries within clients so they can thrive and be their best self.

As a Co-founder NAU Women's Empowerment Jamella is able to offer women a brave space to be transparent, vulnerable, authentic and free with themselves and on another's. The movement help women to gain self-awareness, deepen spirituality, and receive a community of support. Jamella can offer this to women because she received it herself after spending years on her own personal, relational and spiritually developed she was able to find peace and recover from an eating disorder.

You can contact Jamella at
Website: surgeceocoach.com
Email: jamella@surgeceocoach.com

CLARISSA PRITCHETT

Clarissa Pritchett is an Integrative Nutrition Health and Life Coach, Empowerment Speaker, Author, and Army Medical Service Corps Officer. Clarissa is a wife of nine years and mom to three beautiful boys. Clarissa is passionate about health and wellness and has served numerous clients over the past 17 years in the health and medical field. She has a Bachelor's Degree in Health Education, a Master's Degree in Public Health Nutrition and numerous certifications in the fitness and nutrition field. She is the founder of Healthy Family Kitchen and provides women/families with nutrition programs and strong faith-fueled recipes for life. Clarissa is also the founder of Empire Posh Queens and mentors women to start home businesses while promoting Sisterhood, Self-Care, and Service to those in need. She loves to encircle and uplift women to live healthy lives. She has written over 15 fifteen recipe e-books including health and wellness programs. She is a sought- out Speaker and Resilience Instructor for the military, wellness companies, and local churches to share her story of overcoming health/life challenges and to motivate women with their health and life goals. Clarissa is a short, sweet, and spicy mixed salad sistah that keeps it real, raw and organic about how she overcame many health challenges and body issues. Overall, her favorite things in life are Jesus, family, friends, cooking, and eating food, especially tacos, donuts, and chocolate!

You can find more information about Clarissa at: www.ClarissaPritchett.com and treat yourself to some healthy self-care at www.EmpirePoshQueen.com

LINDA ZAMORA

Born in Ruidoso, New Mexico in 1970 to Rolland and Lupe Zamora, Major Linda C. Zamora is older sister to Retired Air Force Tech Sergeant Christina Backus. She started her young life as an "Army brat," traveling the world with her family and eventually following in the footsteps of her father, who retired from military service after two tours in Vietnam and a subsequent 26- year Army career. Major Zamora is the proud mother of Miranda Zamora-Williams, an Athletic Trainer in her second year of her Master's Degree at the University of Wyoming, currently residing in Laramie, Wyoming with her husband Captain Daniel Williams (USAF). She is also the proud mother of Caleb R. M. Affuso, a well-established tattoo artist in Golden, Colorado. Her Grand-dogs are Sushi, Sake and Roe Zamora-Williams and Magnus Nelson-Affuso. Major Zamora is a graduate of Fort Knox High School in Fort Knox, Kentucky, New Mexico Military Institute in Roswell, New Mexico and Eastern New Mexico University. She holds degrees in History and Sociology. Major Zamora is a Military Technician who serves as the Supervisory Staff Administrator for the 372ND Quartermaster Battalion (Petroleum Support) on Kirtland Air Force Base, New Mexico. Concurrently, she is serving in her 28th year of military service as the Executive Officer in the same unit. She is a Bronze Star recipient and veteran of Operation Enduring Freedom Afghanistan. Major Zamora recently opened an urban casual restaurant focused on clean, fresh, vibrant food called Rosemary in Albuquerque, New Mexico.

MEGAN MANIGAULT

Megan K. Manigault, Author, Speaker, and Survivor's Strategist, is passionate about assisting troubled youth and individuals who have experienced traumatic life's obstacles. Megan has always been involved in the community and hopes to encourage others to be the change they wish to see in the world. Through her strategies she's helped many individuals overcome and find the beauty they possess within. When she isn't writing, progressing her mentorship "Infinite Voices", she's working with her new initiative "Thrivers on a Mission", she loves spending time with family and friends. She spends a lot of time learning and researching mental health, business health, and physical health in our communities, so that she can encourage a full circle process to individuals searching for a peaceful, healthy, stress-free life, that's starts with internal development.

MELISSA LYNN

Melissa Lynn is a mother, an entrepreneur, a survivor of abuse, and a self-love advocate. Motivated by her own journey to reconnect with her authentic self, Melissa released 115 pounds of weight that was no longer serving her highest potential. Dropping the stories of her past, she continues to make decisions that align with her own inner peace and happiness. Melissa discovered how to truly find balance and live her healthiest happiest most abundant life possible.

Melissa believes it is her soul's calling to mentor, support, and coach others in finding their own unique path to living a life filled with purpose wellness and happiness. Melissa is a certified Life Coach as well as a certified Nutrition/Health Coach. Melissa is the owner of Lissa Lynn LLC, where she practices a holistic approach to whole-body health and wellness, looking at how all areas of life are connected and how each impacts the other. Contact Melissa for a complimentary discovery session today!

Learn more at www.lissalynn.com
facebook.com/CoachLissaLynn
instagram.com/coachlissalynn

MICHELLE JOSEPH PAUL

Michelle Joseph Paul, was born in Trinidad and Tobago and moved to Baytown, Texas in 1976. She currently resides in Houston, Texas and has 30 years of experience providing human services, to economically disadvantage, populations in the Harris County/Houston area. Ms. Paul holes a Bachelor of Science in Human Service from Springfield College, a Master's Degree in Nonprofit Management for Our Lady of the Lake University and an Evidence Based Coaching Certificate from Fielding Graduate University.

Furthermore, she is a Senior Fellow with the American Leadership Forum, The American Leadership Forum (ALF) is a nonprofit organization whose mission is to join and strengthen diverse leaders to serve the common good.

Michelle's life work is that of service, and from 2011-2013 she worked as a volunteer with The Ultimate Woman Project, a women's empowerment group that was started in her living room when she saw the need for a few of her friends to become liberated from the mental prison of brokenness and uncertainty.

Passionate about her life's work, Michelle founded In-To-Me-See, Inc., to help individuals realize their hearts goals for living as instructed in the scriptural reference of Proverbs 4:23: "Keep thy heart with all diligence because out of the heart flows the issues of life." She utilizes her coaching, facilitating and speaking skills as a conduit for assisting others to live life to their fullest potential.

MICHELLE E. TORRES

Michelle Torres was born and raised in El Paso, TX- a dusty, shabby and romantic city. With a passion for health, wellness, and helping people she graduated from New Mexico State University in 2006 and became a nurse. With a heart to serve her country, she became a military officer in the summer of 2011 in the Nurse Corps. Since moving permanently to New Mexico in 2018, she has deepened her passion for serving God and others in freedom ministry and sharing her story of triumph. She plans to continue to support ministries to end poverty, forced labor, and human trafficking and promote the Gospel of Jesus Christ. She is a woman of faith- a passionate daughter, sister, and friend.

NATALIE BRYAN

From a young age, Natalie Bryan, LCSW has been devoted to serving her community and advocating for others. After completing her B.S. in Interdisciplinary Studies with a focus in Early Childhood and Psychology, Natalie went on to complete her Master's in Social Work at Adelphi University. Natalie has worked in the health and human services field for over 15 years which includes experience in case management, child protective services, mental health clinical services, and working with our veterans. Natalie is also the founder of P.E.A.R.L, an organization that focuses on children and families in our community. The acronym stands for Providing Education and Advocacy to Rebuild lives.

PATRICIA COOK

My name is Patricia Cook. In 1975, I was born in New Orleans, LA, where our culture is surrounded by good food and music. Presently, I live in Moody, AL, which is twenty-five minutes from Birmingham, AL.

Made in the USA
Columbia, SC
12 March 2019